MW00605494

"If you are a student graduating from seminary . . . you need a companion. I have one to suggest. Take Bill Kincaid along with you! Read this book and keep it close at hand. Share and discuss it with your friends, colleagues, and mentors. Kincaid will help you cultivate the curiosity, clarity, agility, proximity, and temerity it takes to flourish in ministry. He is a wise and generous guide."

—**Craig Dykstra**
Duke Divinity School

"In a previous era, pastors could afford to put off bold leadership moves in their congregations until several years into their calls. Today, though, things move more quickly . . . For recent graduates who find this prospect both exciting and daunting, William Kincaid is a wise and humane guide. This book will inspire faithful courage for new pastors as well as those undergoing significant transition in their ministries at any stage."

—**Robert Saler**
Center for Pastoral Excellence

"Bill Kincaid offers a wise and insightful guide for new pastors as they transition from seminary into their ministries. This book is a delightful, dynamic combination of savvy analysis, poetic prose, fresh theological connections, rich metaphors, and vital narratives that unpack the importance and nuances of 'nimbleness' in ministry . . . I intend to give this book to every young pastor with whom I serve."

—**Kim Gage Ryan**
Bethany Fellows and Christian Church (Disciples of Christ) Pastor

"Bill Kincaid brilliantly targets a pivotal time in the life of all new clergy that is often overlooked—the time immediately after seminary graduation when the student becomes clergy. Kincaid offers wisdom in this 'threshold' that is very timely. Our world needs theologically reflective leaders with keen self-awareness and deep spiritual wells."

—Isabel N. Docampo
Perkins School of Theology/SMU

"Had this book been written twenty years ago, it would have saved my colleagues and me many inelegant overturned canoes, but now that is written, every seminary graduate would be wise to read and internalize it when the time comes to approach the water's edge and step boldly into the wondrously buoyant beautiful call of parish ministry."

—Libby Davis Manning
Wabash Pastoral Leadership Program

"*Like Stepping Into a Canoe* is a must read, not only for everyone preparing to enter their first call to ministry but also for those who have served in ministry for decades. William Kincaid beautifully weaves scripture with contemporary, real life situations providing a roadmap for navigating and truly thriving in ministry with nimbleness, curiosity, clarity agility, proximity, and temerity, empowering newly ordained clergy to 'cross the threshold of the transition into ministry worthily.'"

—Ellie Richardson,
Associate Conference Minister, Massachusetts Conference,
United Church of Christ

Like Stepping Into A Canoe

Like Stepping Into A Canoe

Nimbleness and the Transition into Ministry

WILLIAM B. KINCAID

WIPF & STOCK · Eugene, Oregon

LIKE STEPPING INTO A CANOE
Nimbleness and the Transition into Ministry

Wipf & Stock
An Imprint of Wipf and Stock Publishers
199 W. 8th Ave., Suite 3
Eugene, OR 97401

www.wipfandstock.com

PAPERBACK ISBN: 978-1-4982-9847-6
HARDCOVER ISBN: 978-1-4982-4893-8
EBOOK ISBN: 978-1-4982-9848-3

Manufactured in the U.S.A.   08/03/18

Dedicated to the students from my Transitioning and Flourishing class at Christian Theological Seminary, with thanksgiving for the ministry of each one

Contents

Jennifer, Noah and the Transition into Ministry

JENNIFER AND HER SON, Noah, graduated from seminary twenty years apart. While in school they rigorously engaged in their studies of Bible, theology, and history, cultivated meaningful expressions of spirituality, experienced firsthand the joys and challenges of the practice of ministry, and began to articulate and embody their vocational paths with greater confidence and authenticity. After seminary, they both received calls to serve congregations in the Southwest. Their transitions into ministry involved remarkable similarities in some ways, but stunning divergences in others. This is their story.

When Jennifer graduated from seminary in 1996, numerous congregations contacted her with the hope she would become their pastor. Those congregations shared several commonalities. All of them sought a pastor in the traditional sense. "Just come and preach and teach and love us. Help us to experience God's presence and to make God's love real in our community," one woman said during an interview. The congregations all averaged between 125 and 150 worshippers each week. Those sixty years and older represented by far the largest age group in every church that interviewed her. The congregations supported and participated in both local and global outreach causes. The financial support at these prospective churches remained relatively consistent, though all of them would need to reduce the amount budgeted for building maintenance projects in order to offer Jennifer a full-time salary with full benefits.

In other words, though signs of decline and conflict existed when Jennifer graduated, serious questions of survival did not grip the congregations that contacted her in 1996 as she was about to make her transition into ministry. Most seminary graduates of that era moved into relatively stable congregations and into what some have referred to as 'ready-made" ministry positions. Wherever Jennifer might have gone, she would not have been dealing immediately with whether the church would remain open or would close. In most of those communities, the church remained part of a social network that, along with schools, civic organizations, and youth programs, functioned to support what they believed to be the common good of the community and to guard against perceived threats. Being a part of that network may at times have undermined the church's development of a robust Christian identity, but the network generally facilitated helpful conversations about important local issues.

Jennifer visited and interviewed with the four congregations whose values and priorities best matched her own, reaching the conclusion that she could enjoy a fruitful and lasting ministry with any of those four, but she believed God was leading her to Grace Church. Negotiations with the leaders at Grace Church went well and Jennifer began serving there six weeks after her seminary graduation.

Jennifer's son Noah was ten years old when she graduated from seminary. Twenty years later, in the year 2016, Noah graduated from seminary. He also heard from numerous congregations around the time of his graduation. All of them were sought a pastor, but they seemed to want more than a pastor. The congregations averaged between twenty and forty people in worship. Only one congregation could offer what could honestly be called a full-time salary and even it was at the bottom of the denominational scale. That church offered a paltry one hundred dollars per month toward a family healthcare premium that cost nearly seventeen thousand dollars annually. In all of those congregations, he would be the only paid staff. All of them had lost over half of their membership in the last two decades, their buildings were showing extensive neglect, and funds were running out.

The churches where Noah interviewed were located in communities that faced their own stresses. In some cases, a decline in population had led to fewer public services and increased isolation. The towns struggled to channel the energy of an increasingly diverse population into a mutually supportive, mutually appreciative neighborliness. People invested more of their lives in larger, nearby cities, knowing fewer and fewer of their own neighbors and leaving their own communities with a vacuum of leadership. The churches did little to fill that vacuum. Dissatisfaction with the school system became more pronounced, disagreements among residents more dangerous, and depression about the town more obvious.

All of the congregations Noah spoke with had discussed at some point—and usually at some length—whether the time had come to close its ministry and sell its property, but in every discussion someone, much to the chagrin of others, noted that the church just may be on the cusp of finding a new reason for staying around. "The community needs a light more than ever right now and we can be that light," a young man from Word of Hope Church was fond of saying.

Noah heard God's call in the young man's comment and became the pastor of Word of Hope, even though he knew the congregation might close its doors within the year. He agreed to work twenty-five hours per week as pastor, though the salary more fairly corresponded to half that time. He also would work twenty hours each week at a local coffee shop. This offered him the opportunity to make numerous community connections and, not insignificantly, to secure affordable health insurance.

GETTING STARTED

Though making this transition twenty years apart, Jennifer and Noah both experienced relatively early the external shifts that come with many vocations and professional pursuits.[1] For example, they both moved to places where they had not lived before, communities without familiar landmarks or memories. As they moved from being students to being pastors, they adapted to new rhythms and very different work schedules. Elated with even modest salaries and benefits, they now had to manage a new set of economic considerations that included student loans and finally replacing the old cars that had barely made it to graduation day. And instead of talking every day with other seminarians on similar journeys, they now took their place in a different web of relationships that already had a life of its own.

The expectations that the people in their churches had for their new pastors startled Jennifer and Noah. Those congregants did not view Jennifer and Noah as students or learners or even beginners, but as pastors, counselors, community leaders and program directors. It seemed that at least a few in their congregations thought their new pastors emerged from the seminary womb as fully-formed ministers.

Jennifer and Noah began to experience another set of shifts as they settled into their new roles and communities. These shifts felt more internal, having less to do with their new surroundings or with the people they were getting to know and more to do with the way they were viewing and understanding themselves. It's not just that others saw them differently, but that they were seeing themselves differently. Jennifer wondered almost daily, "Who am I to be their pastor? Am I prepared to be their leader? Do I even want to be their leader?" Noah wrestled with another question: "Will they pick up on how lonely and emotionally fragile I am right now?" Both spent a lot of time during their transition into ministry negotiating with their own self-perception while they learned the ropes of being a new pastor.

The excitement of fulfilling a call to ministry and getting to serve as a new pastor carried Jennifer and Noah during most of their first year, but that began to wear off during their second year.

---

1. For a helpful discussion of the external and internal shifts of new pastors, see Scharen and Reed, "Learning Pastoral Imagination."

By the start of year three, they felt restless, unclear and burdened, both personally and professionally, but were not able to identify or describe the specifics of why they felt that way. It was a vague but seriously empty time that left them asking questions that surprised their families and friends. "Did I mishear this call? Am I really cut out for this work?" At one point, Noah announced to his wife that he was going to begin looking for a new job as a website designer.

Jennifer and Noah found themselves struggling to make sense of some very common feelings, but those experiences defied definition and left them questioning themselves and much of what they believed to be true about God, ministry, the church and the world. Often, they assumed that they were the only ones dealing with these relational challenges and internal conflicts.

Jennifer and Noah encountered a web of difficulties regarding transition into ministry that can conspire together to bring even the most gifted and committed new pastor to a moment of deep restlessness and profound reckoning. Those difficulties include dynamics in these five areas.

First, Jennifer and Noah both feared that they were experiencing far fewer opportunities to be creative as they moved from exhilarating spiritual and intellectual encounters in seminary to what they found to be the dullness of the church. Their passion for teaching the faith and caring for others seemed to be undermined by long conversations about a new contract for a copier in the church office and a debate about the dimensions of a new microwave in the church kitchen.

Second, Jennifer and Noah knew the feeling of being utterly overwhelmed. Instead of focusing joyfully on the pastoral work that first drew them to ministry—leading worship, interpreting the faith, caring for others, and guiding the life and mission of a congregation—they encountered an exhausting string of time-consuming distractions and intentionally set diversions that claimed their time and energy. It was as if the church wanted to be anything else in the world except the church.

Third, Jennifer and Noah ran headlong into the deadly intransigence of church systems. An opportunity in Jennifer's community to support the ministry of a nearby homeless shelter got derailed by decision-less and solution-less meetings where people aired twenty-year-old grievances. The indecision, timidity, and exasperatingly slow pace with which church systems act on matters of interest and importance caused both of them to entertain the likelihood that they could best effect change in the world through avenues other than the church.

Fourth, Jennifer and Noah felt an acute sense of isolation and loneliness. They yearned for the early morning prayer group they attended with friends while in seminary. They knew as they approached graduation that they would miss the strong, steady support of their seminary community, but they were still unprepared for the geographical isolation from colleagues and the loneliness that comes from leadership decisions and pastoral situations. Not addressing their personal isolation led to conflict and lack of intimacy with their spouses and children.

Fifth, Jennifer and Noah experienced undue pressure to please others, especially those in the congregation who influence decisions about their employment and the direction of the organization. They wondered why their congregations allowed a couple of families to hold the church mission hostage instead of allowing new ministries to emerge that would bless people in the church and community. The tightrope that new pastors attempt to walk between pleasing a few key people and acting in the best interest of the congregation or agency as a whole can be demoralizing. Despite making occasional progress on congregationally established goals, neither believed their positions were secure. Those familiar with both situations report that Jennifer, as a woman, consistently received less support and more unharnessed criticism than Noah.

THE NATURE OF THIS TRANSITION

The poet Billy Collins says that moving from the title of a poem to writing its first line is a lot like stepping into a canoe. It's tricky and a lot can go wrong.[2]

The transition from seminary into ministry is also like stepping into a canoe. Many early days in ministry feel like we are trying to keep our balance while stepping into a rocking vessel, one that at times seems determined to dump us into the water.

When Jennifer stepped into the canoe, so to speak, it may have rocked a bit, but it felt more securely moored than canoes seem these days. She was able to address the external and internal shifts that new pastors face within a relatively stable environment. The church wasn't without its challenges, but Jennifer and her congregation went about their life together with some comfortable margins. They faced important decisions in the long term, but they enjoyed a window of time, a good reputation, sufficient resources, and a critical mass of gifted people that could have allowed for those decisions to be made prayerfully and deliberately.

Noah, on the other hand, felt waves from deep below the surface rocking against his canoe almost from day one. The tenuous future of his congregation and the increasing discontent and disregard people showed toward their own town created a painful yet amorphous set of issues with which to grapple and address. Though this scenario created great uncertainty for Noah and his ministry, the canoe analogy also saved Noah in some ways. As odd as it may sound, the difficulties he encountered were more easily understood and articulated in the stark realities of the new church and community landscape. As concerned and frightened as Noah sometimes felt, he also experienced a certain freedom by understanding that this canoe-like rocking may be the new normal for the transition into ministry and for the life of the church.

2. "Billy Collins," para. 7.

STAYING ON

The differences did not end once Jennifer and Noah settled into their respective pastoral positions. Both devoted significant preparation time to leading worship, preaching, teaching, and caring for the congregation, but something was being asked of Noah that was not asked of Jennifer. Though they would not have put it this way, Jennifer's congregation wanted a pastor who could manage and maintain. Even though they threw up some early roadblocks, Noah's congregation wanted a pastor who could create and energize. Jennifer's congregation kept an inward focus for the most part, believing that all human and financial resources needed for its mission must be generated from within its own membership. Noah's congregation, in part out of necessity, collaborates financially with an interesting array of individuals and groups in the community who share similar interests and commitments.

Jennifer's congregation often missed new opportunities for ministry by rehashing and second-guessing prior decisions and by propping up long-standing programs that garnered little interest and offered even less impact. Noah's congregation can feel chaotic and scattered, but it exhibits remarkable responsiveness at times. For example, the congregation recently organized a pro-immigration rally on two hours' notice when they learned that a political candidate would be making a stop in their town that afternoon.

Both of these congregations are less well-resourced and well-connected than they were twenty years ago and, barring some intervention, likely will be even less well-resourced and well-connected twenty years from now. Jennifer had one advantage. She could ease a little more gently into ministry after seminary than Noah, who was expected almost immediately to cast a vision and develop strategies that would renew his congregation.

Jennifer's congregation may not have been dynamic, but it was stable. And thus, Jennifer had the indispensable gift of time, which provides the seasoning every new pastor needs to develop pastoral identity, reflection, practice, and imagination.

For Noah and his classmates, the shortness of time served to intensify the five difficulties regarding transitioning into ministry that we have already discussed. This led to some very challenging days in the early part of his ministry. By trying to normalize and even embrace these experiences and not allow them to distract or consume him, Noah steadied the canoe earlier than some of his colleagues.

REFLECTING ON JENNIFER AND NOAH'S
TRANSITIONS

Okay, let's be real about this. I have caricatured some things about Jennifer and Noah. I also have omitted some things from their stories, but the broad strokes of each story convey a fairly common picture. And while your first position in ministry may be a full-time position that reflects more stability than any of those congregations with which Noah interviewed, it will almost certainly look more like Noah's than Jennifer's. Their stories provide several reflection points and touchstones for your own transition into ministry.

Sure, finding the perfect words with which to begin a poem is like getting into a canoe, but isn't that the truth with just about everything we do in life? Getting married is like getting into a canoe. So is having children. Relocating to a new community or beginning a new job are canoes all their own. You are graduating now, but think about when you first came to seminary. Wasn't that something like getting into a canoe?

The transition into ministry is a lot like stepping into a canoe. It is an active, engaged process. Sure, it's tricky, but it is also very doable and very satisfying. I want you to know that now. Stretches of trying to find your balance will give way to seasons of centering yourself in a calling that suits you well. A lot of things can and will go really well. Even a rocky start can develop into a beautiful, enjoyable, and fulfilling voyage. Every pastor and congregation make some mistakes along the way, and both face things that neither can control, but the great majority of missteps and surprises can be folded into everything else that new pastors learn about themselves and about ministry. Each time you get into that canoe you will focus more on the joy of sailing and less on the rocking of the boat. Restlessness never fully goes away, but it gradually gives way to resilience.

And yet, it is a commonly cited statistic that as many as one-third of new pastors leave ministry before they accept a second call or appointment. Some very faith-filled and gifted women and men fall into that category. Some leave ministry because of personal and family circumstances that are beyond their control. Others realize that they went to seminary to explore an important spiritual quest rather than to fulfill a call to pastoral leadership. Some leave ministry for a season or longer and then return, reenergized for ministry and grateful for another chance.

The many who remain in ministry often undergo trials and face serious challenges. Some experience a crisis of faith soon after leaving seminary. Others find themselves at a startling vocational crossroads after investing so much time, energy, and resources in a seminary education. Many report low satisfaction with pastoral ministry at some point during their first few years of ministry. But thankfully, many of those same people find their balance and attain significant levels of fulfillment and effectiveness as they near the end of their first decade in ministry.

Jennifer and Noah faced down the transition into ministry, and that was pivotal. They leaned into the challenges of the transition instead of leaning away. They made friends of these five difficulties rather than enemies, asking almost daily what they could learn from each one about themselves and their ministry.

And they understood well the difference between changes and transitions. We turn to that difference now.

1

Experiencing Changes, Committing to Transitions

MY WIFE AND I learned a lot about changes and transitions when our children began attending cooperative preschool. Every day included numerous interpersonal and environmental changes, beginning with leaving home in the morning and continuing with the various activities of a school day. The kids moved from reading time inside to playtime outside, then back inside for snacks, then from snack time to creative time. At the end of the morning, they said goodbye to their teacher and friends and hello to their mom and dad. They left the classroom and playground of school and returned home to our house and yard.

The children physically moved from space to space, activity to activity, but the transition occurred when their emotional presence and focus caught up with their bodies in their newest location. Their teachers named these transitions for the children, showing them that one part of the day had ended and a new part was beginning. The teacher's gentle but clear instructions helped the children appreciate that an ending had occurred and that the time had come to adjust to the new space or activity. The teacher also let parents know when their children had found some of the transitions difficult. We noticed how our kids became more patient with themselves as a result of this emphasis on transitioning well. And just as the Scriptures promise, our young children led us to think more patiently and creatively about how we experience change and navigate transitions.

People often use the terms "change" and "transition" interchangeably. They will even say, "I've just gone through a transition" when referring to a change in employment or marital status or physical address, but William Bridges contends that changes and transitions are different things altogether. We can experience changes without transitions.[1]

Changes, says Bridges, are the events themselves—the marriage, the divorce, the relocation.[2] We may choose the change or the change may be thrust upon us. Some are nearly imperceptibly small. Others qualify as grand redirections of our lives. We can see some changes coming. Others catch us totally off guard.

Transitions take time. They involve reflection and intentionality. Transitions are the psychological, emotional, and spiritual adjustment to the changes we have experienced.[3] Every transition, Bridges says, involves three phases: 1) an ending where things like a relationship, a job, a life, or a way of understanding has been brought to a close; 2) a neutral zone that surfaces everything from confusion and grief to clarity and anticipation; and 3) a beginning in which a new chapter of life opens.[4] Bridges writes, "Without a transition, a change is just a rearrangement of the furniture. Unless transition happens, the change won't work, because it doesn't 'take.' Whatever word we use, our society talks a lot about change; but it seldom deals with transition."[5]

Your graduation from seminary is a change. If you are among those seeking ordination, that will constitute another change. When you start a new ministry position, that is another change. These are but a few of the changes that you will experience in this

---

1. Bridges, *Transitions*, xii.
2. Bridges, *Transitions*, xii.
3. Bridges, *Transitions*, xii.
4. Bridges, *Transitions*, 17.
5. Bridges, *Transitions*, xii.

exciting and often anxiety-producing season, but remember that these are changes. They are the events themselves. They are not the transitions.

Each change presents the occasion for a life-giving transition, but transitions do not happen automatically. Changes occur all the time to which people do not adjust. We do not make emotional and spiritual adjustments to any new reality simply by plodding through day after day and week after week. Transitions involve prayerful reflection and intentionality. Each change will call for remembering well, letting go, and embracing something new so that you can be emotionally and spiritually present to yourself and to others in the moment and the place where you are physically. How well you transition from seminary to ministry will depend on how faithful you are to the numerous opportunities for introspection and heightened self-awareness when changes occur. Keeping that difference in clear focus will ease your anxiety and lighten your burden considerably during this transition. Losing sight of that difference will complicate your thoughts and feelings and cause you to lose the much needed focus during what should be an exciting time.

Graduating from seminary and becoming a new pastor or therapist or agency director or community organizer is a significant change. We should be careful neither to exaggerate nor minimize it. Understanding its unique features and its commonalities with other life changes will enrich your self-awareness and your ministry. The transition you are experiencing, or are about to experience, needs to be placed alongside other transitions in order to learn from all of them. For example, Bridges cites relationships and employment as two changes that often occur without transitions.

Every relationship of any length will involve numerous changes and, hopefully, many positive transitions, but we know of relationships where change has occurred without the transition. For example, a person looking for a fresh start may change lovers, but then be perplexed when the same issues and troublesome patterns play out in the new relationship. The quick beginning with someone else likely was made to avoid a messy ending and a painful neutral zone of self-confrontation.

Changes and, ideally, transitions occur with our work life as well. Some have lost their employment to the increased capacity of technology and to an outsourcing of jobs to places where the companies will pay a lower wage. Others choose to change jobs within a given field or to pursue work within an entirely different one. Others retire. And still others, like you, might say they were called to a particular vocational path. In each case, an ending means learning to let go in order, over time, to embrace something new. Yet, as with a relationship, without the processing of that ending and the preparing for what comes next, the excitement about a new beginning may wane rather quickly.

Too often, we make changes to avoid transitions.[6] Changes are easier, at least in the short term. Transitions involve slowing down, waiting, and reflecting. Avoiding the dynamics of the transition into ministry leads to a disorientation so profound that new pastors find themselves suddenly questioning their call to ministry. Frequently, the congregation or agency's lack of focus or commitment or spirituality gets blamed for the new pastor's crisis of call, but usually it has at least as much to do—and usually more to do—with the unresolved issues of the transition into ministry.

This book seeks to support your agency and guide your vigorous participation in your own transition into ministry. Other books attend very helpfully to things like how to negotiate the terms of call with a new congregation or how to learn the culture and dynamics of a new community, but these pages are devoted to practices that cultivate your emotional and spiritual adjustment to a transition that may take as long as five to seven years. I am not talking about unpacking boxes and making sure the utilities are connected. The moving truck will be gone within a few hours after it arrives. The ink will be dry on your terms of call rather quickly. You will be fulfilling the pastoral roles almost immediately. But what practices will cause you to adjust emotionally and spiritually

6. Bridges, *Transitions*, 129.

to the larger issues of your transition into ministry? This book focuses on that question.

Let's think now about the endings, neutral zones, and beginnings that are a part of your transition into ministry.

ENDINGS

Let's revisit from the previous chapter some of the endings that Jennifer and Noah faced and then begin to expand the list. These are offered not to discourage or depress you, but to help you understand why you may be so full of emotion and uncertainty.

Like most seminary graduates, Jennifer and Noah left communities where people knew, trusted, and appreciated them. They also left communities they knew, separating from people with whom they had shared moments of celebration and sorrow. While a moment of great joy, their seminary graduation pushed them out of a key community of support. They left behind familiar landmarks that recalled special events and memories. They were both ordained before accepting ministry positions, but they might never return to the holy ground of that sacred ritual. Their many successes in seminary also ended. Jennifer and Noah enjoyed their professors' positive comments on term papers and presentations. Many of the professors repeatedly affirmed their gifts for ministry. Neither relied completely on their professors' emotional support for their well-being, but they did notice and feel the withdrawal when their student days drew to a close and the steady stream of compliments ended.

I have painted the ending of seminary in broad strokes just to capture some of the common experiences. You may have other categories in the ending you are experiencing and your endings most certainly will play out in ways particular to you. For example, you may have despised most of your seminary classmates and held your professors in low esteem, but you are still experiencing an ending with your graduation. That ending calls for reflection and processing.

In finer detail, the endings are too numerous to name. You may be saying good-bye to your child's pediatrician. Your dog may have made her last visit to a familiar groomer. You are moving from a home—whether it is a much loved house or an equally loved student apartment—where you have found refuge and rest during stressful, demanding days. Your driver's license may no longer be effective. Your extended family may now be several states away instead of across town. You eat at the restaurant where you became engaged for the last time. What are the specifics of your endings?

You are choosing some endings and even happy about some, like graduation, but you will experience other endings along the way and they can add up. You may not even realize the emotional impact of some of them until later; Bring them to the surface and, as hard as it will be, welcome their discomfort and grief now for the sake of your transition into ministry.

And remember, you likely are going to a new community or congregation or agency that is experiencing its own endings. If you are becoming the pastor of an established congregation, that must mean that a pastor has left. That represents a significant ending for a congregation. Within a congregation, individuals and families are experiencing various endings. Some have moved and started new work like you have. Others may be dealing with divorce, or helping aging parents move into assisted living, or awakening to the fact that a treasured way of life has ended. In other words, you will live and serve among people who are experiencing their own endings, even as some of yours may still hold an emotional grip on you. Part of entering a new ministry well is to anticipate and be at peace with both the joys and the grief of others while paying attention to your own.

You, too, will navigate the external and internal shifts that most new pastors face. They are part of the rite of passage; that is, there is no getting around them. How you deal with them not only will influence how you view and experience ministry now, but also will set in place some of the habits and attitudes that will characterize your ministry for years to come.

Bridges says that the question to keep before us when an ending occurs is, "What is it time to let go of in my own life right now?"[7] To let go of something does not mean you will disassociate from it completely and erase it from your life. Rather, it can be compared to the cooperative preschool experience of our children. To return inside from the playground and begin reading time didn't mean that they had to forget the fun of playing with their classmates or stop drawing on that joy because they were no longer out there, but it did mean that their emotional presence and focus needed to shift to reading time and the joy it would hold. And I will tell you this: it doesn't matter whether people are enjoying preschool, graduating from seminary or celebrating retirement— those shifts are hard. Even if you are excited about an ending and are absolutely convinced that the path you are on is exactly where you are being led, there is still grief as you disengage from one set of circumstances and patterns. You likely will self-question your own identity as you identify less and less with your seminary community and face some of the other endings mentioned already.

It's no wonder that the transition into ministry is hard. The resulting disorientation[8] exacerbates the difficulties of transition into ministry raised in the previous chapter. You see, sometimes it's not the church that dulls passions and stymies creativity. Some congregations clearly contribute to this, but part of a thoughtful, fruitful transition into ministry involves standing back and reflecting on the endings we have experienced. The disorientation created by a series of endings leaves us unsure whether to trust our own passions and creativity. The same can be said about the seeming inability of new pastors to remain focused on the core work of the pastoral vocation. The tailspin of disorientation creates hesitancy on our part to set and keep clearly defined roles and boundaries. And when the congregation is trying to figure itself and its future out at the same time as the pastor, it's twice as difficult.

Most church systems do not operate with piercing focus and efficiency. We might even debate whether that should be the goal.

7. Bridges, *Transitions*, 128.
8. Bridges, *Transitions*, 121.

What seems likely is that we will view the church's intransigence more harshly because of our own disorientation.

In any time of grief it's not unusual to seek time alone. Part of the isolation new pastors feel comes from the need and desire to make sense of the recent endings. And yet, most new pastors do not have extended periods to grieve before they are plunged into the relationships and issues of a new congregation or agency. Again, ministry brings various dimensions of isolation and loneliness. Rather than feel guilty about wanting time alone or worrying that the isolation will deaden your soul and doom your ministry, consider the other option. The time alone during your transition into ministry is a way to honor and be realistic about the endings you have experienced. If you can receive alone time as a gift rather than as a personal or pastoral deficiency, you will know that you are progressing through your transition into ministry.

The disorientation can leave you terribly vulnerable when dealing with the pressures and expectations of other people. We can find ourselves looking to others to remind us who we are and even to inform our values and commitments. While learning from each other is a good thing, mooring ourselves to those who wish to control us as pastors and people leads to disaster. A time of disorientation can result in porous boundaries and manipulative relationships on everyone's part. This doesn't mean that we remain so guarded that people cannot get to know us and trust us, but it does remind us that it is better to grow relationships appropriately rather than to go too deep too early and be left with the usually hopeless task of trying to reset some very loose boundaries.

The endings described here are both personal and pastoral in nature. You have experienced a number of endings as you begin your transition into ministry. This is a time to be good to yourself and those nearest you.

How well you attend to the personal dimensions of your endings not only will enhance your own well-being, but also will contribute to the ease with which you navigate your transition into ministry. Further, if you negotiate the personal and pastoral aspects of your endings well, the congregation or agency that you serve will begin to manifest signs of your clarity and strength.

NEUTRAL ZONES

A young person in a church where I once served received many job offers when he graduated from a top flight engineering school, including a job with a world-renowned consulting firm. He accepted that firm's offer and began negotiating the details of a contract, saying he would really like a week off after graduation and before starting this new position. "You'll get more than that! We don't want you showing up tired from your studies with your mind still spinning from college. You'll start in October." And with that, the new employee was sent off on a four-and-a-half-month transition period.

Now, here's the downside. When he finally began work, that company nearly worked him to death. They practically owned him. It's a good thing he got to play and travel from mid-May to October, as once that transition was over, he had to consistently spend weeknights at the office, take phone calls on the weekends, and forfeit vacation times.

Even with that downside, however, he was given that rare opportunity to begin something new after he had spent time renewing himself and processing the ending of his college career. He was thrilled to have graduated, but it was still a change, and with change comes the need to end well and prepare emotionally and spiritually for what comes next.

Sharing this story generates mixed feelings for me. On the one hand, if you want that kind of time between seminary and a new ministry position and have the means to support you for four and a half months, I hope you get it. That in-between time could prove helpful in coming to grips with changes and moving through transitions, but I've never known a minister who was given that option. Most seminary graduates need to move quickly from seminary student to being a new pastor and make that new beginning before they have processed some of the endings in their lives.

Unfortunately, the church doesn't always recognize and affirm the many gifted seminary graduates who are prepared and eager to lead and serve. Some have to wait even longer than four and a half months to begin their ministry. Waiting on a call after graduation is often only the latest discrediting of their personhood, gender, race or ethnicity, and call to ministry. In this case, perhaps people have grieved and prioritized in preparation for a new beginning that has not yet come, which can cause a whole new round of endings of expectations and plans.

Listen to how Reverend David Shirey described his changes and transitions while moving from a congregation in Arizona that he had founded to a historic church in Lexington, Kentucky. He captured this experience well when he wrote this letter to his new congregation:

> Dear Friends,
>
> I'm glad to be here, but I'm not here yet. I've been in Lexington 27 days now and am delighted to be here . . . but I'm not here yet. Please bear with me as the rest of me arrives from Phoenix over the next weeks and months. The rest of me includes all my stuff—all Jennie's and my worldly belongings that are back in Phoenix waiting to be loaded into a moving van. Our stuff will follow. We hope. I'm tired of wearing the same outfits. We've been living this month out of a suitcase in our hotel. Once the moving van arrives within a couple weeks, we'll move into our new home. But there's more of me that's not here yet than furniture, books, and clothes. There's a 12-year investment of my heart, mind, and soul that is still out west. I'm well aware of the baggage I did bring across country and have been carrying with me these first weeks in Lexington—a measure of grief. It, too, will pass. In time. The depth of it is a measure of the love I developed for those dear folks at Coolwater Christian Church. In time, I will develop that same love for Central Christian Church and for Lexington. Count on it. I'm a pastor at heart. I love people. Especially God's people.

That means you. I'm glad to be here, but I'm not all here
yet. But I'm coming. Thank you for your patience as my
stuff . . . and my soul . . . make the move.[9]

Like David Shirey, you likely will start a new position in
ministry before your neutral zone ends, which means that you will
want to carve out time so you can continue to process the ending
and prepare for the beginning that is already under way.

What do you want from your transition? What do you want
to be able to say that you have learned as a result of this transition?
What healing will you seek? What will you celebrate and anticipate? What will you do differently as you begin something new?
Keep these questions in front of you. Find times and spaces when
you can entertain them honestly and assess whether you are getting what you need from the transition.

The traditional wisdom for the transition into ministry is
that time is your friend. Most new pastors will develop an effective pastoral voice and imagination if given enough time and if accompanied by gifted mentors who can reflect with them at critical
junctures and events. That's true, of course. The key to forming a
life-giving pastoral identity and practice is the gift of time.

But many who are reading this book are going into situations
where there does not appear to be a lot of time. In cases where the
congregation or agency is in steep decline, or perhaps even the
whole community, the window of time in which stability can be
introduced and vitality renewed is usually quite short. Even those
ministry situations that continue to exhibit relative strength likely
need to be discerning how to extend their life cycles so that they
will continue to express their faith and commitments in each new
season and circumstance.

In other words, the transition into ministry involves a lot of
dynamics. You will be emotionally processing several endings, all
while a new beginning is already taking shape. Just being in transition is hard work. It's no wonder that on some days you will have
little energy left for anything but tending to your own emotions.

9. Shirey, *Chimes*, 1.

At the same time, you also will find yourself on a shifting landscape of church and ministry that brings its own pressures and threatens to crowd out time to reflect and prioritize. New pastors always have gone through stages of developing their pastoral identity and practice through the weekly rhythms and surprises of ministry, but the gift of time has been in more plentiful supply in prior seasons than it is now. Opportunities to stand back and reflect on the dynamics will not come naturally. You will have to create intentional, regular space to identify and articulate the particular dynamics with which you are dealing and to consider how best to care for yourself and those closest to you and to set healthy patterns for your ministry.

Because your seminary graduation and your start of a new ministry position likely will occur in very close proximity to one another, you will be confronted with the challenge of sorting out the emotions of the neutral zone and the emotions of the new beginning. It will be hard to get off to a good start in a new congregation or agency without cultivating relationships in your new setting. At the same time, few temptations are greater in the transition into ministry than quickly replacing the old relationships with a whole set of new ones. Whatever we have lost, we try to replace quickly.

Few of us enjoy emptiness. It makes us so uncomfortable that we try to shorten the time between our endings and our beginnings. In other words, we squeeze the neutral zones into the shortest possible amount of time and, in doing so, we move on to what comes next without giving prayerful consideration of our life's last chapter. We keep at bay hard questions, especially those that leave us feeling vulnerable and inadequate.

There will be days when you feel hemmed in and stymied, days of being overwhelmed and frustrated, days of dancing between feeling isolated and wanting to be alone. Bridges says that we should stop trying to escape the emptiness of the neutral zone. Instead, he urges us to surrender to the emptiness and aloneness so that we can embrace the reparation, renewal and reintegration that comes from sobering, enlivening introspection.

The neutral zone is a time to celebrate the good of our endings, acknowledge the grief involved, and determine what matters enough to us to move forward with it.[10] We can't live in the neutral zone forever. We need more certainty than that, but we can't live well in other stages and seasons without the healing and fertile reflection that occurs in the neutral zone.

BEGINNINGS

The transition into ministry begins with a series of endings in which you think about what you need to let go of, then moves into a neutral zone of grief, reflection, and prioritization, and finally culminates when you are emotionally present and focused in your new beginning. It's the new beginning that completes the thoughtful, intentional transition process. You awake one day to realize that you are living in this new beginning in ways that you have long imagined to be at your core. Your call to ministry takes on confidence, clarity, and concreteness. Because of your act of letting go and reflecting in the ending and neutral zone stages, respectively, you are free to begin and begin well. Your transition into ministry culminates with the beginning of a new ministry.[11]

As Bridges so simply puts it, "you finish with a new beginning."[12] That sounds counter-intuitive, but the transition nears a fulfilling completion when you begin to live well and confidently in your new ministry position. The challenge to completing your transition into ministry will be remaining present and honest with the spiritual and emotional changes that you are encountering in each stage of the transition. We tend to grow impatient with

10. Bridges, *Transitions*, 147.

11. Though not common, in some cases graduates may continue in the same ministry position after seminary that they had during seminary. In those cases, changes still occur. Processing those changes will be essential to a fruitful transition into ministry.

12. Bridges, *Transitions*, 157.

the pace that it takes for our feelings to catch up with our bodies. That's what David Shirey is saying in his letter: "I'm glad to be here, but I'm not all here yet." We want to rush ahead to the new beginning without taking into account the stress and strain of the changes. And as we have already discussed, some of these changes are ones we are eager to celebrate, like graduating from seminary! Still, it takes most of us a while to process the changes, and without that processing, the new beginning—no matter how much it is anticipated—will not go as well.

Beginnings can be exciting. They are fresh and new. The possibilities seem endless at the point of a new beginning. Beginnings also can be overwhelming. We can find them intimidating and loaded with the potential for mistakes. The key question for your new beginning in ministry is this: what is waiting in the wings of my life to make its entrance?[13]

You are making the transition into ministry at a particular moment with a particular set of circumstances. The landscape on which you are beginning your ministry looks quite different from the landscape over which those who graduated from seminary embarked even fifteen years ago. As a result, you probably have heard a few discouraging words about what lies ahead for you and the church. In many cases, congregations and agencies are smaller and are attempting their ministry with fewer resources. The church often has succumbed to the temptation of self-preservation instead of offering itself in love and service to the world. The gospel temperament of adventure and boldness has given way to caution and timidity. The network of partners upon which the church drew in previous generations has not evolved into new collaborations. And in the end, this often has meant fewer ministry positions, or ministry positions that provide less compensation and opportunities for joyful impact.

It's true that an already tricky transition has been made trickier because of the changes and pressures that congregations and agencies are feeling, but it's also true that an incredible array of opportunities exists for new ministers who can engage situations

13. Bridges, *Transitions*, 87.

with confidence and scrappiness, ask probing questions, work with interesting and diverse partners, take a few risks, make some worthwhile mistakes, and above all, stay close to what caused you to enter ministry in the first place. Opportunities abound to bless and positively impact congregations, agencies, and communities. Today's expressions of vitality and renewal in the church may not always look like they once did, but they are present and real. Good news can be found in a variety of settings and circumstances. You are graduating from seminary at an exceptionally exciting time to be doing ministry.

Three dynamics, in particular, will help you make sense of this new beginning. First, you should be aware of a common refrain of new pastors: "I feel trained, but not free." New teachers, attorneys, social workers, and physicians, just to name a few, make similar comments. "Trained but not free" describes people in various fields and vocations who have not yet been able to translate their excellent training into a fully expressed practice and performance. Often, the training leaves them with a lingering sense of timidity, unable to look up from a script that they are not sure even exists. They fear making mistakes, so they become uptight and anxious about the very thing they love, as if they are holding on too tightly. They come to resent the thing that once brought them the greatest joy. This is part of completing the transition into ministry and there's really no way around it. The freedom comes from remaining engaged in your new ministry, consistently doing the work that is at the core of the pastoral vocation, and reflecting on your life and work with a seasoned pastor, counselor, or coach. This dynamic is a sign that your new beginning is underway. The path to feeling both trained and free runs directly through the week-to-week ministry in which you are now involved.

You may think of yourself as a new pastor who is transitioning into ministry, but people in your congregation or agency simply think of you as pastor or executive director. They acknowledge on some level that you are relatively new to ministry, but their expectation for faithful leadership and guidance is not put on hold for five to seven years while you figure everything out. Nor can the needs of a congregation or agency in crisis or decline be delayed. And if the people with whom you serve do view you as a new, inexperienced pastor, take advantage of that! That likely means they will be quite forgiving in those moments when things don't go well. What they probably won't excuse is you doing nothing.

Second, many transition-into-ministry mentors and programs have argued that there's really no substitute for time when it comes to the transition into ministry, but that wisdom comes with some qualifiers. Some of you will begin ministry positions where, as noted with Jennifer and Noah's story, there does not appear to be much time. The decline is steep and the grief is deep. But even in the best circumstances, time is only your friend in the transition into ministry when it is used well. This is not time observing and waiting; you can only learn so much from watching. The well-intentioned posture of being a friend of time has resulted in too many new pastors in the early years of ministry getting separated from the very call that brought them to ministry in the first place. That is not the intention of the transition into ministry wisdom, but it has played out this way. New pastors, already carrying with them the timidity of being "trained but not free," interpret the need for time as a reason or perhaps an excuse to set aside their passion for the gospel and their pastoral leadership. Instead of leading with that passion, new pastors concede leadership opportunities to others and frequently accept identities and roles that a dysfunctional congregational system all too eagerly, yet quite insidiously, assigns to them. This results in a debilitating lack of fulfillment, the kind and degree of which contributes to a high rate of attrition among new pastors.

Third, as counter-intuitive or even absurd as it may sound, today's church and ministry challenges provide just the opportunities you need to develop as a new pastor. The transition is still tricky, but the very things that make it tricky also will provide you with some of the best and most important learning you will ever know. Your rigorous engagement in ministry, including your missteps, will accelerate your learning and cause you to prioritize your ministry in helpful ways.

You will complete your transition not by withdrawing until the storm passes, but by stepping into the opportunities to practice a creative, faithful ministry in the midst of the storm. I am referring principally to the many shifts in religious and social life occurring in the United States at the moment, but also the inner storms you are experiencing through this transition.

Those who tentatively move into ministry or resist the learning opportunities will make their transitions more difficult, not less. In effect, their tentativeness stretches their transition into ministry, causing it to last longer than it otherwise needs to and, in some cases, making new pastors feel like they are always transitioning and never really moving on to the next season of ministry. They likely will get caught up in the impulses and rewards of congregational systems, losing sight of their vocational core as pastors. As a result, they will find themselves increasingly distanced from the passions that first fueled their call to ministry. This contributes to the isolation pastors often feel and can foster a death-dealing resentment that makes creative, enjoyable ministry nearly impossible.

On the other hand, new pastors who vigorously engage the possibilities and uncertainties during the transition into ministry are far more likely to launch a pastoral career characterized by positive impact and profound fulfillment. They will have learned far more, gained greater personal and professional resilience, found a new level of confidence, believe more deeply in the value of their ministry, and embody a greater sense of anticipation for the next chapter of their life and work in the church and community.

The patterns that pastors embody across the seasons of a ministerial career begin to get set during the transition into ministry. It's much easier to develop healthy and effective patterns early in your ministry that will sustain you across many seasons than it is to recover from unhealthy habits and practices halfway through a ministerial career. That wisdom applies to practical things like time management, but just as importantly, it applies to the pastoral temperament. If timidity is encouraged and coveted during the transition into ministry, leading courageously later on will be hard to do. I bet your call to ministry excited you in ways that few other things have. My guess is that your call to ministry did not sound much like minding the store and maintaining the status quo. More likely, your call probably grew out of your concern for God's people and God's world and was further animated by the opportunity to help others experience the same faith in which you have found new life. If that is the case, don't leave that calling behind and don't get disconnected from it. This is the adventure for which you have waited and worked. Attempt imaginative, joyfully impactful ministry even now, during your transition into ministry.

People facing new beginnings encounter both the exciting and the overwhelming in abundance. This includes new pastors who have graduated from seminary and are about to start a new ministry position. What helps focus anyone moving through the final stage of a transition is to align their inner lives with the work of the new beginning, stay close to their passion and enthusiasm, prepare to act in their new role and setting, and begin seeing yourself living and acting confidently in ways that express your calling as a leader and pastor in this new beginning.

And remember the good news. None of this happens outside of God's comforting, life-giving presence. Not the ending, not the neutral zone, and not the beginning. We turn to that good news now as we develop a theological framework for our understanding of transitions.

2

Knowing God's Presence, Trusting God's Leading

THE WORLD IS AND always has been in transition. Consider the sweeping transition captured in the Bible between two gardens. An ending occurred in Genesis 3 when God sent humans away from the Garden of Eden.[1] The book of Revelation, with its position as the last book of the Bible, usually gets interpreted as an ending, that moment when God's purposes prevail on the earth and history as we know it is brought to a close, but what if the promises of Revelation 21–22—the promise of a new heaven and a new earth—are actually a beginning that renews creation and causes us to see afresh the beginnings all around us? The promise in those last two chapters of the Bible help us to reject death-dealing ways and cause us to look now, in the time in between the gardens, for the tree of life that produces fruit and leaves for the healing of the nations.[2]

We live our lives as part of larger changes and transitions around us, caught up in the history of humanity and God's transforming vision for the world. A world of vocation exists in the

1. Gen 3:23.
2. Rev 22:2.

midst of that sweep, calling us through exhilarating opportunities and heartbreaking situations to participate in God's healing and restoration. And in the midst of that vast sweep and the grand vision of God's ultimate purposes, we live our individual lives and perform our ministries in the midst of numerous personal and social changes. With the excitement, uncertainty, and grief come these questions: where is God in the midst of change? How do we understand God's presence when we are moving through endings, neutral zones and beginnings? And how have people understood and grappled with God's purposes when the outcome of change is unknown?

CHANGES AND TRANSITIONS IN SCRIPTURE

Let's begin by looking at stories of change found in Scripture. None of these stories have been preserved in Scripture to support the theory of transitions, but we see movements within each story that are instructive for our thinking about change in general and the transition into ministry, in particular. The first shows the problems that can result from a quick accumulation of changes with seemingly no spiritual and emotional adjustment. The second one describes a transition that someone believed needed forty years to fully transpire. The third one offers a model worth considering for those who seek an enjoyable and lasting transition.

For our first story, consider some events from King David's life as recorded in 2 Samuel 11. The king had sent the officers and soldiers of Israel out to destroy some neighboring tribes, but he remained in Jerusalem. A beautiful woman who was bathing across the way caught the king's attention. David might have looked away, or might not have requested Bathsheba's presence, or might have restrained himself in some other fashion, but none of that happened. Instead, changes began immediately and one change quickly led to another.

The king had Bathsheba brought to him and before very long she became pregnant. At that point, David could have shifted into a neutral zone to evaluate what had happened and to imagine a better way forward. He could have confessed what he had done and caused no further pain or damage. Instead of pausing for reflection, David quickly begins something new in this tragic story. He calls for Uriah, Bathsheba's husband, to make love with her so that Uriah might conclude that he is the father of the baby. When that doesn't work, David gives orders to place Uriah at the front of the worst fighting to ensure his demise. In other words, rather than stepping back, interrupting this cycle of events, and learning from a terrible mistake, David rushed in to make an equally horrific second mistake. By Bridges's terms, David made several changes, but made them in such rapid succession that the emotional and psychological growth of a transition never developed.

Such exaggerated moves and high stakes nearly make this story too absurd to be instructive in the transition into ministry discussion, but perhaps the extreme relief in which this story is cast will be helpful during the questioning, discerning days of concluding your seminary studies and beginning a new ministry. You likely won't send any armies off to war, and you probably won't be on your church's roof and have somebody on another church's roof catch your eye, but you will make mistakes. I have made them. Everyone has made them. In every case, some of the subsequent and more serious lapses could have been avoided by stepping back and evaluating the situations rather than plunging quickly into the next decision or action. At some point, as with David, rapid, successive changes can send us and those we love and lead into a spiral from which it is difficult to escape.

Second, consider the story of the Exodus, an event that remains central to the Jewish faith and continues to be told down to this very day on the first night of Passover. The Exodus offers a paradigm by which we can think about various liberation movements. Where the story about David offers an overstated lesson in what not to do, the Exodus story falls so neatly into Bridges's categories that we might imagine that the Hebrews navigated through these stages more easily than they actually did.

The story begins with an ending. We see signs of that coming ending in Exodus 2 when a new king, one not acquainted with

Joseph, began to rule over Egypt. He quickly expressed his concern that the Israelites had become more numerous and more powerful than the Egyptians. The fear that the Israelites would seek to overthrow Egyptian rule, either on their own or by joining with one of Egypt's enemies, led the king to intensify the slavery and oppression in which Egypt held the Israelites. The Israelites, though, continued to grow in number, which caused the Egyptians to grow in fear, dread, and an attitude of scarcity.[3]

Signs of the ending continue to be seen in Exodus 3 when God speaks to Moses in the burning bush. "I have observed the misery of my people in Egypt,"[4] God says. This moment of calling kick-starts the ending. And this is the way the ending is remembered and recited even now: "By God's mighty hand and outstretched arm, the people were liberated from slavery." Slavery in Egypt ended with the Exodus. That was the change.

But the beginning did not occur right away. The transition occurred over the next forty years—and perhaps longer—as the Hebrews adapted psychologically and spiritually to no longer being enslaved. That experience cannot be easily overcome. The Hebrews did not move immediately from one ending to a new beginning, but rather spent forty years in the wilderness making that adjustment in what Bridges calls a neutral zone. And, as you probably remember, the transition did not come easy.

> The whole congregation of the Israelites complained against Moses and Aaron in the wilderness. The Israelites said to them, "If only we had died by the hand of the LORD in the land of Egypt, when we sat by the fleshpots and ate our fill of bread; for you have brought us out into this wilderness to kill this whole assembly with hunger."[5]

3. Brueggemann, *Journey to the Common Good*, 7.

4. Exod 3:10.

5. Exod 16:2–3. The Exodus story frames the nature of transitions because of its pronounced stages—Egypt, wilderness, and Promised Land—but transition stories can be found throughout Scripture. It can even be argued that the biblical story itself is one grand transition story as all creation lives somewhere between the Garden and the New Jerusalem.

Freedom from Egypt was the change. The wilderness represents the neutral zone that is critical for the transition to continue. They did not need forty years to make that trip, but they needed at least that much time to rid themselves of the identity and mentality of slavery. The Promised Land represents the new beginning.

You may only move a few miles when you begin your new ministry, but the emotional and spiritual adjustment will occur over a much longer period of time than the time it takes to drive or fly from the seminary to your new church or agency. You will not have forty years. You'll not even receive the four months that the young man did that I mentioned in the previous chapter, so begin thinking now about the intentional wilderness that you will seek so that you can make sense of the changes that are going on in your life right now. We tend to think of the wilderness as something to avoid, but if you will remember, the Spirit led Jesus into the wilderness.[6] It's likely that your transition into ministry already feels like the wilderness, at least on some days, but perhaps because of the over-functioning that occurs among new pastors you are resisting the wilderness or not able to see its value. If it was valuable for Jesus' own identity, focus, and mission, we should probably pay attention to that. In between time, whether we call it wilderness or neutral zone, it is not wasted time. It gives us space for Spirit-led reflection and discernment.

Third, consider the hopeful story of the Council of Jerusalem in Acts 15, a story that points to both a significant change and a healthy transition. Gentile Christians no longer had to be circumcised first in order to follow Jesus and join the church's fellowship. This change of direction makes some of the contemporary church's debates and divisions seem like child's play. A change like this could have resulted in a severe split of the early Christian community, but instead it opened doors for the church to embrace more people.

In this case, a change took place. A position on gentile Christians ended, but with that ending a marvelous transition actually begins back in chapter 10 of Acts. The transition unfolds over

6. Matt 4:1

several chapters as an ending occurs, a discernment-rich neutral zone ensues, and a new beginning gathers much-needed traction and energy. The church would encounter other challenges later and bring a few of them on itself, but this moment situated at the center of the Acts of the Apostles frames for us a useful and hopeful transition.

If you track this transition through the book of Acts, you will notice that it took time. It took a lot of time and a lot of patience. The leaders negotiated and renegotiated positions. They sought clarity and direction by revisiting prior conversations and engaging in new ones once they became aware of unanticipated implications. In this way, the story of gentile inclusion in the early church provides a model for your beginning. You are beginning something that will unfold over years. You cannot squeeze every question or concern into your first three months of a new ministry position. Jesus said that today's concerns are enough for today. No need to import dilemmas and conflicts from the future. Allow yourself some space. Trust that time well-spent engaging ministry, reflecting on that ministry and learning about yourself will be your friend. Be patient with yourself in this new beginning. And remember, this is the start of your ministry. This is your beginning. It's something to enjoy and then, at some point, to look back on fondly.

GOD'S PRESENCE IN TIMES OF CHANGE

God is always present to us and that is no less true during change than at any other time. The psalms affirm God's presence in the midst of change: "though the earth should change, though the mountains quake in the heart of the sea; though its waters roar and foam, though the mountains tremble with its tumult . . . God is in the midst of the city . . . the LORD of hosts is with us; the God of Jacob is our refuge."[7]

7. Ps 46:2–3, 5, 11.

In another place, the psalmist announces God's inescapable presence.

> O LORD, you have searched me and known me.
>   You know when I sit down and when I rise up;
>   you discern my thoughts from far away . . .
>   You hem me in, behind and before, and lay your hand
>   upon me . . .
>   Where can I go from your spirit?
>   Or where can I flee from your presence?
>   If I ascend to heaven, you are there;
>   if I make my bed in Sheol, you are there.
>   If I take the wings of the morning and settle
>   at the farthest reaches of the sea,
>   even there your hand shall lead me,
>   and your right hand shall hold me fast.[8]

What is true of all those changes that the psalmist mentions—sitting down, rising up, ascending to heaven, making our bed in Sheol, taking up morning wings to settle at the farthest reaches of the sea—is true of the changes you are now experiencing during your transition into ministry. God is present to you. Your changes are occurring within the flourishing life God wills and gives to all of creation. In every moment, "we know that all things work together for good for those who love God, who are called according to his purpose . . . If God is for us, who is against us? . . . in all these things, we are more than conquerors through him who loved us . . . [because nothing] will be able to separate us from the love of God in Christ Jesus our LORD."[9]

The assurance of God's presence comforts and encourages us, but God also can be a discomfiting presence. Just ask Jonah.

> Now the word of the LORD came to Jonah son of Amittai, saying, "Go at once to Nineveh . . . and cry out against it; for their wickedness has come up before me." But Jonah set out to flee to Tarshish from the presence of the

8. Ps 139:1–2, 5, 7–10.
9. Rom 8:28, 31b, 37, 39b.

> LORD. He went down to Joppa and found a ship going
> to Tarshish . . . away from the presence of the LORD.[10]

Jonah was ready to get away from it all, including God. First we have to ask the following question: where did Jonah think he was going? When Jonah decided to flee the presence of the LORD, just where did he have in mind to go? No boat sails that far. Tickets cannot be purchased for such a destination. Jonah knew what it was liked to be hemmed in.

Then we have to ask this: what are your Nineveh and your Tarshish? And what are mine? What issues and challenges are emerging during this transition into ministry that cry out for attention and work? Chances are that they are the same issues and challenges that we either confronted or chose not to confront during previous changes in our lives. Does Nineveh represent some lingering wound or harmful pattern that we are turning away from because addressing it will be tiring and time-consuming? Does a trip to Tarshish appear to be a way to avoid dealing with a painful wound, destructive pattern, or messy ending? And do we make that trip even if it threatens to undermine our well-being and our ministry?

Or does Nineveh represent accomplishment and success that you fear? Marianne Williamson says, "Our deepest fear is not that we are inadequate. Our deepest fear is that we are powerful beyond measure. It is our light, not our darkness that most frightens us."[11] Perhaps you are avoiding Nineveh because you are uncomfortable with God's light shining through you and your ministry. Maybe you are hesitant to step into the public eye that pastoral leadership involves. You may be trying to avoid being associated with the sometimes-empty expressions of success in American culture and want to distance your ministry from those measurements. Whatever your reservation might be, God is relentlessly persistent in calling and equipping people for ministry. If you are going to

---

10. Jonah 1:2–3

11. Williamson, *Return to Love*, 190–91.

end up in Nineveh anyway, you might as well start in that direction now.

The extent to which you make peace with the inescapable presence of God will determine the level of joy and fulfillment you know during this transition. It is, after all, this same God from whom you received this calling and who has sustained you thus far on this path. The transition into ministry is an opportunity to turn toward God, not away. The psalmist says that even when we turn away, we turn toward God.

And yet, a difference exists between not being able to escape God's presence, on the one hand, and being able to recognize and appreciate its embrace on the other. Like fish and water, God's presence is our truest habitat, our truest surrounding, our home. I hope your transition into ministry does not include "hardship, or distress, or persecution, or famine, or nakedness, or peril, or sword,"[12] but even if it does, none of those things have the power to separate you from the love of God that we have come to know in Christ Jesus. I encourage you to claim that assurance all through your transition into ministry, including those days when, thanks be to God, there is no real hardship or distress or persecution in your life.

God's constant presence instills peace and brings perspective when navigating change. That peace and perspective causes us to be more generous and patient with ourselves first, and then with others. Take the time to delight in the ways God's grace envelops you and those close to you during the many goodbyes and hellos of this change.

God is present to you, guiding and strengthening you during this transition, but God also calls you to think beyond your particular transition to the rich possibilities and, yes, challenging circumstances that you will encounter in your ministry. Remember, very soon after Moses experienced the radiance of God's presence on holy ground, God sent Moses to liberate the people from slavery in Egypt. Revel in God's presence, knowing that God will continue to call you to a ministry of healing and hope.

12. Rom 8:35b.

GOD'S GOOD DESIRE FOR THE WORLD

God's good intent is at work amid every change and transition. That's true whether we are talking about the early church discussing its membership rolls or about you making the most of the current changes in your life. God works for good even in the most troublesome and perplexing changes. We live in the midst of these changes with backlit eschatology, as Matthew Myer Boulton puts it.[13] In other words, we are already walking in the light. God's promises are trustworthy and our lives show forth that light to the world.

"God has a dream for the world," says the website of Christ Church, an Episcopal cathedral in Lexington, Kentucky. The message continues, "Cathedrals exist to give us a glimpse of that dream." I would argue that there are more things than just cathedrals which exist for that purpose, but the point remains the same. Cathedral or storefront, inner-city or rural, or anywhere in between, whatever the racial and ethnic makeup, whatever the family of faith or the style of worship or the organizational structure, individual Christians and Christian congregations exist to give the world at least a glimpse of God's dream and to beckon us to engage in the hopeful, practical realities of making God's dream real, visible, and concrete in the world. "Your kingdom come, Your will be done, on earth as it is in heaven," as Jesus invited us to pray while working alongside him.[14]

Or, as Wendell Berry puts it:

> You work always in this dear
> Opening between
> What was and is to be . . .
> The slow song
> Of the great making, the world never
> At rest, still being made.[15]

13. Boulton, *Life in God*, 144.

14. Matt 6:10.

15. Berry, *This Day*, 124, 385.

Catholic priest and poet John O'Donohue describes this emerging transition as a "genesis foyer." He captures the way change develops into a transition by saying it's the moment or place "where something that not yet is might begin to edge its way from silence into word, from the invisible into form."[16]

Sometimes what is to be is very slow in appearing. Much of the time we trust in God's blessings and the fruit of our labors as we midwife the world's renewal, and God's dream for the world lives within us and around us, even if the edging into reality is painfully slow. You see, your transition into ministry is not the only transition that is taking a while to unfold.

And what is that world that is slow in emerging? What is that dream God has for the world?[17] Jesus succinctly announced, "I came that they may have life, and have it abundantly."[18] Jeremiah puts it just as clearly: "For surely I know the plans I have for you, says the LORD, plans for your welfare and not for harm, to give you a future with hope."[19]

Marjorie Suchocki says that "there is a locus for justice in the nature of God."[20] From that locus emanates the divine mandate in Isaiah: "I have called you in righteousness . . . I have given you as a covenant to the people, a light to the nations, to open the eyes that are blind, to bring out the prisoners from the dungeon."[21]

GOD'S BECKONING AND OUR RESPONSE

God beckons all of creation to live well and to serve the just causes that support flourishing communities. So, while God accompanies you through these changes from seminary to life and ministry beyond seminary, God also calls you even in the midst of the change

16. O'Donohue, *To Bless the Space*, 23.

17. Tutu, *God Has A Dream*. The dream imagery of God's desire for the world is found throughout this book.

18. John 10:10.

19. Jer 29:11.

20. Suchocki, *God, Christ, Church*, 78.

21. Isa 42:6–7.

to ministries that bring dignity to humanity, build up the church and renew creation. In other words, while this book focuses on the particular issues of your transition into ministry, this is not a private journey that is only concerned with your individual well-being. We are ultimately addressing our relationship with God and paying attention to how God leads individuals and communities of faith to work within changes and transitions to bring about good.

This beckoning God sides with the suffering while at the same time nurturing in us an adventurous faith that seizes possibilities to bless the world. After all, God does not just beckon once, but in every season and circumstance, time and time again, always with the hope that we will join God in facilitating healing and cultivating the abundant way.

We are called to participate in what God desires for the world, not against God and not against ourselves, as so often happens in the transition into ministry. Just as we all are becoming as individuals and pastors, the church is always becoming as well, responding ever more attentively and faithfully to God's leading. At its best, the church begins to see not with human eyes, but with the eyes of God.[22] In doing so, possibilities and promises come into view, even in the midst of change and transition. As William Stafford put it, "Your job is to find what the world is trying to be."[23]

Admittedly, it would be nice if God faxed or tweeted a few more specifics, pointing us unquestionably in the direction we need to go and toward the problem we need to solve, but as Marjorie Suchocki writes, "If love always looks to the real needs of the other, then love cannot predetermine what those needs will be, and how those needs will be met."[24] Perhaps the WWJD bracelets aren't as helpful as WWJG—where would Jesus go. Jesus said, "Whoever serves me must follow me, and where I am, there will my servant be also.[25] Participating in God's purposes in the world means being present where Jesus would be present and, you may have noticed,

22. 2 Cor 5:16.
23. Stafford, *The Way It Is*, 102.
24. Suchocki, *God, Christ, Church*, 97.
25. John 12:26a.

he spent a lot of time with people experiencing change and going through transitions.

Nimble pastors draw on the rich theological consciousness cultivated in seminary to interpret the presence and purposes of God in the world. This is the first work of ministry. They lead worship, teach the faith, and care for the congregation, but they also go about their work with a keen eye for possibilities where others see only neglect, gridlock, and hopelessness. They pursue these possibilities with a scrappy temperament that refuses to believe that things cannot be better. For them, grit and persistence are as essential to ministry as grace and respectability. These leaders demonstrate the kind of nimbleness needed to broker partnerships, seize opportunities, think beyond institutional maintenance, and empower communities of faith to enact justice and facilitate healing. Day after day, these church and community leaders engage their ministries with creativity and imagination.

Your transition into ministry happens within many contexts—your personal and family life, your pastoral style, and your church structures, to name a few—but the larger context for your transition into ministry is always the world's transition as God continues to call forth kindness and justice for all of God's children. I do not intend to diminish your transition into ministry, but rather to invite you to situate yourself and your transition in the larger narrative of God's redeeming love and to guard against the transition-into-ministry trap of an ever smaller frame that includes only you and your well-being.

Where is God in the midst of change? Present. Present to you and me and the world that God loves so much.

But God is more than simply present. God calls to us to recognize that we live between two gardens. Though the transition brings challenges, God continually holds before us life and death, blessing and curse, and then encourages us to choose life, over and over, and to participate in its most abundant expression.[26]

Perhaps the following hymn captures it best:

26. Deut 30:15–20.

You call from tomorrow, you break ancient schemes,
From the bondage of sorrow the captives dream dreams;
Our women see visions, our men clear their eyes.
With bold new decisions your people arise.[27]

27. Manley, "Spirit," 249.

3

A Time to Be Nimble

LEWIS, A GRADUATE OF the seminary where I teach, recently reflected with me on his time in school and his first few years in pastoral ministry.[1] He reminded me of a comment he made in a leadership course before he graduated. Lewis began the class discussion that morning several years earlier by saying, "I completed the assigned reading and I think I understood what I read. And, well, this isn't what I signed up for." He paused when I asked him what he meant by that comment, but eventually continued: "This is too risky. I don't want to put myself on the line like this with a group of people."

It was unusual for Lewis to talk this much in class. The reading obviously had connected with him, though not in the way I had hoped when I made the assignment. He stared at the floor for a minute and then said, "I'm just looking for a position where I take care of the people and the church takes care of me."

I asked, "But wasn't your decision to come to seminary a risky one?"

1. This story arises from a series of interviews that I conducted over a period of ten years with alumni from Christian Theological Seminary in Indianapolis. I have altered some details in order to preserve the person's identity, but the essence of the story remains intact. I share this story with the person's permission, and they agree with the way that I have characterized their journey.

"I suppose so."

I looked for ways to keep the conversation going and to keep Lewis from shutting down. Someone seeking to avoid risks in ministry probably wouldn't be too keen on an emotionally charged class discussion. As I thought about how best to raise the next question, another student jumped in. "How do you avoid risks when following Jesus?"

"I manage."

"Or in your marriage?" another student chimed in. Lewis sat with his arms folded, signaling to the class that he had said all he was going to say.

I might have understood Lewis's position better had he been transitioning into ministry now instead of many years ago. Now, religious, cultural, economic, and political trends continue to evolve and evolve quickly. Divisive forces eagerly and effectively work against common ground and common pursuits. Contextual shifts, congregational dynamics, and an upheaval in pastoral roles add pressure to a new pastor's life. The gift of time that we claim works best for the development of new pastors is at odds with what many new pastors actually experience in the churches and communities where they serve. Too many new ministers are not getting to enjoy and take advantage of the reflective seasoning that occurs in the first decade after seminary due to the demands placed on them.

But Lewis graduated at a time when numerous opportunities existed to serve in relatively stable congregations and communities. Lewis began serving as a pastor just a few weeks after graduating from seminary, but he left ministry after three years at that church. He then worked for an insurance company for four years. When I interviewed Lewis seven years after his seminary graduation, he was seeking to regain his ministerial standing with the Presbyterian Church USA.

"Can you point to two or three things that became the key factors in your decision to leave ministry?" I asked.

"That's easy. Caution. And maybe it's more like fear. It's driven my life. Going to seminary was by far the most adventurous thing

I've ever done. I still haven't recovered from the ways I was challenged there."

"How did your caution play out when you were leaving seminary?"

"In everything. I mean, relationships, that's one. I didn't initiate any relationships with people except in pastoral care situations. The congregation had some opportunities to expand their ministries with things that likely would have brought in more people, but I remained distantly silent when the congregation discussed those possibilities. And most of all, I turned my back on my own growth and learning."

And then it happened. He said, "Do you remember that morning in class when I said I didn't want to put myself out there? I said that what was being described in that book sounded too risky."

I told him that I did. I added that I thought he was particularly self-aware during that conversation and that I still appreciated his openness and honesty all these years later.

"What I said that day probably doomed my transition into ministry." Lewis went on to describe that he had approached the move to his first church after seminary tentatively and even reluctantly. He wondered if perhaps he had been depressed and didn't realize it, but for the most part he simply followed the same patterns he always had. The people of the congregation had welcomed him warmly. The church had grown in membership and financial stability before his arrival, largely due to an automobile manufacturer relocating to the area only a few years earlier. The town where he lived was safe, convenient and pleasant. In other words, things were in place for a fulfilling and enjoyable ministry, but Lewis did not engage. Relationships withered before they ever got started. Possibilities for further church growth waned. And the more cautious Lewis became, the less likely he would ever gain traction for his transition into ministry.

Numerous well-meaning reasons exist for easing gently and slowly into the transition into ministry. For example, just like other vocational paths, it takes time to understand what you are really supposed to be doing as a pastor. Plus, you might make mistakes. Or you might overcommit yourself at times. Or you might harm someone with poor counsel. Or you might lead a congregation or agency astray. And so, the result often is that people will wait until that magical moment when they have it all figured out and then at that point persuasively and passionately apply what they have learned.

All these "mights" get in the way of your call to ministry, how you will approach your pastoral leadership, the positive impact your ministry can have, and the exciting and important learning that will occur if you engage now. These "mights" contribute to a timidity that will be hard to break free from later.

You begin setting patterns for your ministry from the very first day. One of those patterns is your own temperament. It's not helpful to pretend you will be more engaged or more adventurous or more courageous later on.

Now is the time to stay connected to your call to ministry and those you seek to bless through it. Now is the time for you to value your call and see its God-given importance so that hesitation and busyness do not distract you. Now is the time to engage in truly rigorous on-the-job learning for the sake of the church or agency that you serve, but also for the sake of your own pastoral journey and those purposes of God that matter most to you.

A TIME TO BE NIMBLE

If nowhere else, you have heard the word "nimble" associated with Jack, as in "Jack be nimble, Jack be quick." It's often characterized as swift dexterity, but it means more than just reacting or moving quickly. The term these days is used often to describe leaders and organizations whose decisions and actions flow from a high level of focus, readiness and agility. The lack of nimbleness causes organizations and businesses to lose their competitive edge and their market share. For example, numerous department stores with long histories have closed or greatly scaled back their operations because of online competition and nimble niche retailers.[2] Rather easy comparisons can be made to the church and its sluggish response to the evolving context in which it lives and offers ministry.

I am arguing for an understanding of nimbleness that will allow you to address head-on the five key issues regularly found in the transition into ministry. Over time, the congregation or agency that you serve likely will begin to reflect your clear and courageous leadership.

Nimble pastors stay close to emerging possibilities, identify opportunities that others either miss or ignore, and stand hopefully in the midst of difficult conversations, all for the sake of those who need to know God's kind and relentless love for the world. Nimble pastors and flourishing congregations look beyond self-imposed limits and draw on resources that have gone unrecognized in the past, often because we in the church simply are not programmed to spot what is right before our eyes or because we are, for various reasons, reluctant to ask for support and to cooperate with others. Resources and networks exist; they just may not be the ones to which churches have traditionally looked. Through new partnerships and fresh resources, many wonderful ministries are blessing individuals and communities with life-giving encouragement and tangible uplift.

For example, some pastors are scrambling to plant new congregations while employed full-time in other work. Others are renewing sluggish and dying congregations through small satellite missions in their city. Still others are establishing community advocacy groups that are making public transportation and employment more accessible. Whether beginning something new or renewing something old, the once dependable resources and networks often cannot and, in some cases, choose not to support these efforts; yet these ministers continue undauntingly to pursue an adventurous path in birthing a new ministry for the sake of hurting individuals and struggling communities.

2. As one example, this is how J. C. Penney described its decision to close up to 140 stores and eliminate six thousand jobs in its announcement on February 24, 2017.

New pastors who simply want to go to a church and preside over things will find that, by the time they have figured out what they are presiding over, everything will have changed. New pastors who want to sit in their study and wait on the action to come to them will experience a lot of loneliness and irrelevance.

The narrative of decline that has become so prevalent in church circles only tells part of the story. Some congregations are hunkering down and even hibernating, but many are engaging the realities of their contexts in hopeful and constructive ways. It is true that some are grief-ridden and anger-filled, but many are bringing hope to forgotten neighbors and abandoned neighborhoods.

While some are lamenting changing demographics, others are learning radical hospitality. While some are wringing their hands at the ravages of poverty and absentee property owners, others are making micro loans to support social enterprise and neighborhood well-being. While some are lashing out at those they call different, others are confessing their racist attitudes and living in reconciled relationships.

While some grow increasingly nervous about their communities, others work with various partners and agencies to eliminate widespread drug trafficking and gun violence. While some feel cheated that the latest pre-packaged church program didn't attract hordes of new members, others form intentional communities of study, protest, fellowship, prayer, and Eucharist.

As exciting as all this is, I realize that at this point you may still be thinking about the canoe. You may be asking, "Am I expected to engage the most challenging situations that the church and community face while I negotiate this tricky transition into ministry?" Or you may be protesting more vigorously and more loudly. "No! I can't be thrown into a situation like that. Don't you understand, I'm just starting out! I need time to figure out what I am doing."

Let's be realistic. You may prefer to ease away from the shore by yourself as the sun rises and the birds sing, spending the morning sailing gently on still waters, but it is quite likely that you are already out on a stormy lake with a canoe full of people who want to know how you are going to calm the choppy waters and restore yesterday's tranquility. You may or may not have oars at your disposal. And if you do, you may or may not be allowed to use them. I appreciate your desire to move cautiously and even guardedly into this transition, but learning and engaging the particulars of your ministry setting will lead to a far more enjoyable and fulfilling transition.

Think about the nimbleness of Jesus. Jesus is always pivoting from person to person, from opportunity to opportunity, from need to need, from teaching and healing to retreating and praying and back to teaching and healing.

Think about how the gospel of Mark begins. Jesus moves from being baptized by John, to receiving God's affirmation, to being driven immediately into the wilderness where he knew both temptation from Satan and the comfort of angels. When he emerges from the wilderness, he at once invites Simon and Andrew to follow him and immediately calls James and John to do the same. The action continues to unfold quickly as Jesus teaches and heals in the synagogue. Then, they all had barely left the synagogue before they enter the house of Simon and Andrew, where Jesus caused the fever of Simon's mother-in-law to leave. By nightfall, everyone in Capernaum gathered around Jesus to see what diseases he would cure next. Then, in the darkness of early morning, Jesus went out to a deserted place and prayed. As the sun came up, he and his relatively new followers headed for the neighboring town of Galilee and another day of pivoting and transitioning from one situation to another.

All this happens in the first chapter of Mark, and words like "immediately," "straight away," and "just as" remind us that these transitions often carry some urgency. He was responding to a need in some cases. In others, he was moving toward an opportunity.

What informs and guides the pivots that Jesus makes? We might respond with, "He was the Son of God (or, God the Son) and so he knew exactly what lay ahead of him and how he would respond." This fits, of course, especially since Mark begins (1:1) and very nearly ends (15:39) his account with the announcement that Jesus is, indeed, the Son of God. But Jesus does not often demonstrate that kind of omniscience in the gospel of Mark and typically refers to himself as "the Son of Man." We see him move nimbly from person to person, from community to community, from circumstance to circumstance. He exhibits curiosity by asking great (and sometimes annoying) questions. He shows clarity by always pointing people toward the realm of God in their midst. He demonstrates agility as he pivots from situation to situation. In a memorable moment of proximity, he remains so close to people that he put his fingers into a deaf man's ears and touched his tongue.[3] And we see his courage as he engaged powers and principalities with a gospel of compassion, justice and hope that did not remain theoretical. Jesus did not express support for these things alone and then stand back, hoping someone would act on these central principles. Rather, compassion, justice, and hope guided Jesus' life and ministry, and his nimbleness caused him to embody these things everywhere he went.

To transition and serve with nimbleness means that you will be making pivots of your own. There's nothing sedentary about impactful ministry. Sitting in our study looking distinguished may give us short-term pleasure, but it's not going to bless many individuals and communities.

So what will inform those pivots during your transition into ministry and beyond? What do you believe so strongly or care about so deeply that it will keep you pivoting toward a truer and more compelling expression of your call to ministry? When you first recognized a call to ministry, to what adventure did you think you were responding? That adventure still calls to you now as you begin your ministry, urging you to venture out and engage whatever it is that God and the world have for you. Jesus consistently pivoting toward the realm of God in our midst is our pattern, our encouragement, to pivot toward the realm also.

These are the questions to keep before you. The status quo will come at you full force with its busyness and distractions, inviting you to duck things that really matter and to look away from

3. Mark 7:31-37.

the world's hurting and most vulnerable people. Just keeping an institution alive, even if it is the church, isn't a good enough reason to maintain something that no longer holds meaning or supports mission. Often, in the interest of survival, people stop listening for God and stop noticing their neighbors. Maggie Barankitse's description of her work is unforgettable. In describing what caused her to respond to the slaughter of the Burundi Civil War with a network of services for children, she said simply, "Love made me an inventor."[4] Who or what do you love that much? How will that love propel you into a ministry that makes love visible, concrete, and impactful?

In the ninth chapter of the Acts of the Apostles, Ananias expresses his hesitation about being sent to visit the recently converted Saul and to lay hands on him so that Saul would regain his sight. "But LORD, I've heard all the evil he has done to your saints in Jerusalem," Ananias begins. God reiterates, "Go." And the reason God gives is that this man named Saul is going to be an instrument chosen by God "to bring my name before Gentiles and kings and before the people of Israel."[5]

It causes us to ask of ourselves, "For what reason or for what purposes will we be an instrument?" Few things motivate and sustain the pivots of a transition like being able to discern, articulate, and claim for our living the answer to that question. Every time you pivot toward these purposes of God during your transition into ministry, you become a little more of an instrument. Every time you pivot away from those purposes or don't pivot at all, you slow down your transition into ministry and create patterns that will hinder your chances of becoming an instrument for God's healing of the world. That may sound blunt, but it hopefully makes it clear that a fruitful transition into ministry depends, in large part, on your active, intentional engagement.

---

4. Quoted in Byassee, *Trinity*, 91. For more information about Maggie Barankitse's courageous humanitarian efforts in Burundi, see "Love Made Me an Inventor."

5. Acts 9:15.

THIS IS NIMBLENESS

Nimbleness, as shown in the diagram below, is the interaction between five practices—curiosity, clarity, agility, proximity and temerity. I will introduce each practice here and then go into more depth with each one in the following chapters. We begin with curiosity.

We practice curiosity when we have an appetite for the new and an appreciation for going into more depth with the familiar. I am reminded of the Godly Play approach to worship for children. At the end of each story, the children and the storyteller are encouraged to make "I wonder" statements. Curiosity reflects and cultivates wonder and awe in one's life. Questions allow us to see and experience the world differently.

Probing questions lead not only to discoveries, but also to more probing questions. Seminary nurtures a desire for the big questions of life and faith, but also for interests and topics outside of ministry that will assist you in living a whole life. New pastors experience energy and vigor when this desire carries over into the transition to ministry. Asking only timid and utilitarian questions during the transition into ministry can shrink one's spirit.

We practice clarity when we decide how we will be instruments and engage the vocational core of being pastor. Ministry with congregations and community agencies often involves the approach of a generalist who handles a range of roles and responsibilities. This already makes pastoral work challenging at times as we seek to give appropriate time and energy to those various roles and responsibilities. Numerous other requests on the pastor's time, some of which have little to do with the work of being a pastor, further complicate pastoral work. Nimbleness does not mean we say yes to everything. Just as congregations and agencies need guardrails in order to stay focused on their mission, so pastors need guardrails in order to prioritize and execute their work. One's ordination vows or one's job description provides this focus, but new pastors especially find it hard to build their weeks around those priorities and find it even harder to say no when requests come. As a result, pastors often do not deliver the needed leadership and frequently are disconnected from their particular gifts and passions. Heightening one's clarity during the transition into ministry develops a strong foundation for the seasons of ministry that will follow.

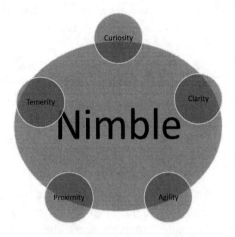

We practice agility when we demonstrate a temperament for adventure and respond hopefully and concretely to opportunities. Nimbleness is not reckless reactivity or even spontaneous agility by itself. It's not just reactionary agility that scurries to pull things off at a minute's notice just because something happens to present itself. The challenge is that most congregations and agencies are not built for agility. They have learned to institutionalize rigidity and, as a result, their ministry gets reduced to propping up structures. They become captive to those structures, even obsessed with them, and they forget that their work is to bring light and kindness and justice to the world.

Agility can be measured in readiness. Is this congregation ready to act—or could it be ready to act in short order—if an opportunity that is consistent with its mission presents itself? Is this agency able to respond to a need when it arises in the community? The people of one congregation described their agility as scrappy elegance. By that, they meant that they understand that the ministry of the church cannot always wait on us to get every little detail in the right place and with a lot of polish. Your practice of ministry will become increasingly refined over time. You will forfeit opportunities if you wait until you are perfectly polished before you act.

We practice proximity when we stay close to what matters to us, to what is emerging in the community, and to a network of collaborators who share similar values and commitments. This means paying attention to our own well-being, the family members with whom we are making this journey, and the specific ways our faith informs and prioritizes our ministry. To practice proximity positions us to strengthen the present life of a congregation or agency, as well as to look toward its horizon for what comes next. At the same time, the proximity of our ministry connects us to the current conversations and events in the broader community as alliances address important issues like education inequity, substandard housing, and public transit. Proximity often evolves into hosting occasions for the broader community to discuss, discern, and implement strategies for the benefit of those who have been abandoned and forgotten. Proximity accelerates learning during the transition into ministry. Backing away from issues, situations, and possibilities slows down learning.

The practice of temerity is the practice of nerve and courage. This isn't grandstanding, and it's not a power grab. Temerity empowers us to stay close (proximity) to what matters to us and the community and to act (agility) for the sake of the broader good. A good place to start is simply by doing what you have been called and authorized to do by virtue of your ordination vows and the terms of your call.[6] All these years later, I still think about what drove people to risk their lives marching from Selma to Montgom-

6. I understand that not everyone reading this book is seeking ordination or is already ordained. This may be because some church traditions do not ordain ministerial leaders at all, or because ordination is not open to you in your church tradition, or because your discernment has not led you to make yourself available for ordination, or because the work you are doing does not require or involve ordination. In those cases, think in terms of your job description with the same clarity, asking this question: "What lies at the heart of my work, and how does the allocation of my time and energy reflect piercing clarity about that work?"

ery, Alabama in 1965. I think about the physical and emotional abuse those marchers endured on the Pettus Bridge, and I am moved still by their temerity. At the same time, we exhibit temerity week after week in lesser known places every time we faithfully preach and teach about the justice of God. We demonstrate nerve every time we contribute constructively to difficult conversations and decisions. We show courage every time our yes is yes and our no is no.[7]

Nimbleness is the interaction of these five practices. When one practice is missing, nimbleness is diminished. Without clarity of purpose, for example, we may display frenetic reactivity or allow lesser motivations to guide our decisions. For example, someone who feels pressure to please others likely will take on more tasks, not fewer. Or, someone who already feels loneliness might actually find a strange solace in a slow-moving church system that craves togetherness over accomplishment. You can see how someone's transition into ministry can stall as a result of these issues, or worse, get completely derailed.

When the dynamics of those five practices is missing, the shadow side of these elements will undermine one's ministry and diminish one's capacity to effect change. You may find it helpful to look at the diagram again and imagine different practices being shown as significantly smaller circles as a way to represent what happens when one of the practices is missing. For example, without clarity our agility becomes reactivity that jumps from one mission to another without anything serving as a guide. Without agility, all the clarity in the world remains inactive. Without proximity, our temerity never gets involved in concrete situations. Without temerity, our clarity and proximity are wasted. And without curiosity, a beautiful world becomes dull to us, resignation sets in, and nothing changes.

7. Matt 5:37.

JENNIFER AND NOAH'S NIMBLENESS

Unlike Lewis, Jennifer and Noah found that engaging these five practices helped them make sense of their transitions into ministry and caused them to find their pastoral voice much sooner. It wasn't always easy, but when Jennifer and Noah felt their passions dulled and their creativity stymied, they found ways within themselves and beyond the congregation to keep their curiosity alive. When they became overwhelmed by the barrage of tasks and the demands of congregants, they used those moments as clarifying filters through which they could remain focused on the core aspects of their pastoral vocation. When they and the congregation got hopelessly stuck in their own tracks, Jennifer and Noah articulated possibilities toward which the congregation could pivot and regain momentum for its mission. When they experienced the isolation and loneliness of ministry, they made sure their relationships with their spouses and children remained strong while also modeling community engagement for their congregations. And every time—well, at least most of the time—people in the church and community subtly encouraged them to step back from the most pressing issues, they pushed forward, meditating on a verse of Scripture they had recited since Noah was in youth group: "For God did not give us a spirit of timidity, but of power and love and self-control."[8] The more they enjoyed their ministry, the more their congregations exuded a spirit of joy and generosity.

In short, Jennifer and Noah got to a new beginning, and when they did, they engaged these core transitional issues with nimbleness. Each practice addresses an issue that new pastors deal with during the transition from seminary to the ministry that comes after seminary. These practices are intended to break down the transition into manageable areas so that more and more new pastors can make the same decision when they get to a new beginning.

> For the dulled passions and the stymied creativity, the practice of curiosity.

8. 2 Tim 1:7.

For the barrage of tasks that muddles the pastoral vocation, the
practice of clarity.

For the intransigence of church systems, the practice of agility.

For the isolation and loneliness, the practice of proximity.

For the work of the gospel and the expectations of others, the
practice of temerity.

Nimbleness is the vigorous engagement that is essential, especially in today's context, for a fruitful transition into ministry.
Each aspect of nimbleness receives an in-depth discussion in the
chapters that follow. Together, these five practices cultivate a focused ministry and an adventurous temperament now, when you
need it the most, giving you greater learning and clarity about your
pastoral work and leading to more satisfaction and impact in your
ministry. This is a time for church and community leaders to be
nimble, even if those church and community leaders, like you, are
just beginning their pastoral careers.

Nothing can replace the poignant, piercing poetry of Ecclesi-
astes 3, but for your transition into ministry, perhaps we can think
of this as a pastoral supplement.

There's a time for the tried and true and there's a time for
imagination.

There's a time for general enjoyment and there's a time for piercing clarity.

There's a time to preside with distinction and there's a time to
engage scrappily.

There's a time to be cautiously distant and there's a time to be
daringly close.

There's a time to prayerfully discern and there's a time to courageously act.

There's a time to be sure-footed and deliberate and there's a time
to be nimble.

And this is the time—not later, not when you think you will have it all figured out, but now—to be nimble.

4

Curiosity

How can you be sure that ministry is your vocation? I can only offer this conjecture. Something's your vocation if it keeps making more of you.[1]

O Holy Spirit, visit my soul and stay within me all day. Inspire all my thoughts. Pervade all my imaginations.[2]

"When you wake up in the morning, Pooh, what's the first thing you say to yourself?"

"What's for breakfast?" answers Pooh. "And what do you say, Piglet?"

"I say, 'I wonder what exciting thing is going to happen today?'"[3]

Possibilities are because God is.[4]

---

1. Godwin, *Evensong*, 12.
2. Baillie, *Diary of Private Prayer*, 83.
3. Milne, *Winnie-the-Pooh*, 160.
4. Suchocki, *God, Christ, Church*, 80.

JENNIFER CHARACTERIZED THE SPIRITUAL and intellectual encounters in seminary as exhilarating. They evoked a creativity in her unlike anything else she had experienced before, but by the end of her first year in ministry she felt her imagination almost completely squelched by what she viewed as mundane and immaterial conversations in the church. Her mentor asked her why she was allowing a few conversations to quash her interests in a world infused with wonder and human connectivity. The direct question caught her off guard at first, but she couldn't set the question aside because it struck at the heart of her dilemma.

Jennifer started creating liturgical pieces occasionally and inserting them into her congregation's staid order of worship. The congregation responded with appreciation and anticipation. She realized that the congregation was much more curious and open to newness than she assumed. Later, she realized that most of her congregation had never visited the Grand Canyon, even though they lived less than a four-hour drive from it. Jennifer organized the first of several trips and experiences, including some to the Grand Canyon, to keep wonder alive for her and her congregants. In her third year at the church, Jennifer began participating in short-story writing workshops hosted by the public library. These and other initiatives, all spurred by Jennifer's curiosity, put patterns in place both personally and pastorally that renewed her creativity and kept her in touch with the wonder that stirred in her during her seminary days.

CURIOSITY AS A PRACTICE

Wonder holds a central place in the Christian story, yet it often fails to get expressed in the life and work of the church and its leaders. For example, hear again the soaring words of the psalmist:

> O LORD, our Sovereign,
> how majestic is your name in all the earth! . . .
> When I look at your heavens, the work of your fingers,
> the moon and the stars that you have established;
> what are human beings that you are mindful of them,

mortals that you care for them?[5]

And

> How lovely is your dwelling place,
> O LORD of hosts!
> My soul longs, indeed it faints
> for the courts of the LORD;
> my heart and my flesh sing for joy
> to the living God.
> Even the sparrow finds a home
> and the swallow a nest for herself.[6]

And

> Every day I will bless you,
> and praise your name forever and ever.
> Great is the LORD, and greatly to be praised;
> his greatness is unsearchable.[7]

The songs of the contemporary church also invite us into a renewed dimension of wonder in our life and faith. For example,

> Womb of life, and source of being,
> Home of ev'ry restless heart
> In your arms the world awakened;
> You have loved us from the start.[8]

And

> Praise to the LORD,
> Who doth nourish thy life and restore thee,
> Fitting thee well for the tasks that
>   Are ever before thee.
> Then to thy need
> God as a mother doth speed,
> Spreading the wings of grace o'er thee.[9]

---

5. Ps 8:1, 3–4.

6. Ps 84:1–3a.

7. Ps 145:2–3.

8. "Womb of Life, and Source of Being," in *Chalice Hymnal*, 14.

9. "Praise to the LORD, the Almighty," in *Chalice Hymnal*, 25.

And

> Thou reignest in glory;
> Thou dwellest in light,
> Thine angels adore thee
> All veiling their sight;
> All praises we render
> O help us to see
> That only the splendor
> Of light hideth thee.[10]

Imagine a God who reigns in glory over the heavens and the earth, yet provides a home to every restless heart and responds with tender grace to every need. What could be more wonder-full!

Wonder is woven through every dimension of the Christian story, but the church and its leaders often gather, worship, study, and serve with a wonder deficit. This makes the transition into ministry particularly difficult as new pastors seek to experience in ministry the joyful stirrings and fulfilling moments that first led them to consider this vocational path. And often, because processing changes and transitions can be so emotionally draining, new pastors look to those in their congregation or agency to exhibit wonder in their faith. In fact, sometimes new pastors depend on others to demonstrate noticeable wonder, and when others don't do so in response to what new pastors deem to be an acceptable level, the new pastors criticize the people rather than reflect on their own wonder deficit. The strategy for lamentably discouraging moments is to step back from the inclination to blame someone else, breathe in God's care for you, and reacquaint yourself with wonder in your own life and faith. Doing so will inspire wonder in others far more effectively than judging the spirituality of the people around you.

Curiosity addresses the stymied creativity and the wonder deficit. Every question unlocks possibilities and unleashes talents and energy. Paths open, ideas synergize, perspectives coalesce, and gifts mobilize all at the sound of a question.

---

10. "Immortal, Invisible, God Only Wise," in *Chalice Hymnal*, 66.

What is true of the world is equally true of you and me and anyone else who is or ever has been a new pastor. We change at the sound of the first question, and the more we practice curiosity, the more we grow, evolve, and develop during this transition.

Of course, there's far more to being curious about than just Scripture, theology, hymns, and the practice of ministry. Wonder pulses around us as we walk in the woods and stroll on beaches. Wonder encompasses us when an infant wraps her hand around our finger, as well as years later when that one-time infant walks across a commencement stage or down a wedding aisle. As Maria sang, "The hills are alive with the sound of music, with songs they have sung for a thousand years. The hills fill my heart with the sound of music, my heart wants to sing every song it hears."[11]

And then there is the wonder of holy ground, of standing on sacred earth where the just and peaceful purposes of God came alive in the course of history. When my class and I stood at the foot of the Edmund Pettus Bridge in 2015 on the fiftieth anniversary of Bloody Sunday and saw a President Obama-led symbolic march across that bridge, I really didn't know whether to cheer or cry, so overwhelming was the moment. I'm afraid the wonder of it all may have overcome me so that I stood there silently and just watched.

I encountered a similar experience on a visit to South Africa. We traveled with the well-known anti-apartheid leader Dr. Allan Aubrey Boesak and visited with Archbishop Desmond Tutu. Those experiences alone made for an amazing trip, but few things have sparked wonder in me like visiting St George's Cathedral in Cape Town for an early morning liturgy. In addition to St George's being the seat of the bishop, it also is the site where numerous anti-apartheid protests were held and from which many marches began. The direction of history changed in South Africa, and the epicenter of that change was arguably St George's Cathedral. As I worshipped that morning, I felt surrounded by a great cloud of witnesses who had gathered as a community week after week, sung the faith, listened for a word from the LORD, received the Eucharist, and then risked their lives for the sake of a fairer, more just nation. Wonder

11. Rodgers and Hammerstein, "Sound of Music," 1965.

enveloped me as I thought of those people and participated in the liturgy. The experience also reminded me that in lesser known places, the same gathering happens over and over, and sometimes we miss the wonder of those moments that are occurring before our very eyes.

John Calvin was concerned with how the wonder of faith deteriorates into dullness. We fail to delight in the works of God "in this most beautiful theater"[12] that is the world around us, but it doesn't have to be this way. "The numbness of oblivion," wrote Calvin, "[can] give way to the vivid, quickening sensation of life."[13]

John O'Donohue invites us into the next step: "What is the new horizon in you that wants to be seen?"[14] In other words, the wonder doesn't just envelop us, it also rises within us, spurring our imagination and positioning us for discovery. This is the practice of curiosity and it keeps us alive to the beauty and possibilities in places and seasons where our spirits might otherwise dry up and blow away.

Numerous schools, organizations, and companies test for what is known as the curiosity quotient. Some say this is at least as important as intelligence.[15] The imaginative spirit and the hungry mind animate people, nurture problem-solving, and cause us to see things others might miss.

Curiosity appears as the first practice in this list of five because it has the capacity to propel you into the other four practices and through your transition into ministry. Barry, for instance, describes curiosity as what fuels his ministry.

> I try to encounter something every week that heightens my curiosity because it helps me push through the physical and emotional fatigue of the transition. Much of what sparks my curiosity isn't directly related to church and ministry. Recently, I've been learning how clocks work. Before that, I read several biographies of U.S. presidents.

12. Boulton, *Life in God*, 109.

13. Boulton, *Life in God*, 110–11.

14. O'Donohue, *To Bless the Space*, 5.

15. Chamorro-Premuzic, "Curiosity."

Curiosity is intended to broaden your interests, not create more work for you or lead to over-functioning. New pastors, understandably, want to show that they can do this work. They don't want to leave anything undone that falls to them, but since they often aren't clear exactly what falls to them (the chapter on clarity comes next), they often do far more—and with greater intensity—than they will do when they appropriately focus their pastoral practice and settle into their pastoral identity in later seasons of ministry. If you are like most new pastors, you will spend a lot of energy trying to exceed expectations and protecting yourself from criticism. Curiosity gets squelched as a result.

Anxiety in the church or agency you are serving can squelch curiosity as well. As we've already noted, many new pastors will be going into lean situations where the window of time is short and a scarcity mentality has set in. It will be difficult for you not to absorb some of the accompanying anxiety. That anxiety acts as a barrier between the people and their own faith story, a story that frequently announces "Do not be afraid"[16] and "I am with you always."[17] Moseley and Lyon remind us of the paradox that in times of change and loss, we seem unable to access the resources of our own faith story.[18] It's no small task for an individual, especially a new leader, to practice curiosity in the midst of pools of anxiety and grief.

How you balance your current emotional needs with setting your long-term patterns for ministry will decide how healthily and effectively you will move through this transition and into subsequent seasons of ministry. So, while caring well for yourself in these early years remains a priority, significant attention needs to be paid to a vision of ministry for yourself in which you are always asking generative questions that no one else seems to be asking, pressing beneath the surface of conversations to get to the real issues, and pursuing angles and depths that feed your spirit

16. Matt 28:10.

17. Matt 28:20.

18. See Moseley and Lyon, *How to Lead*, for a helpful discussion of this.

and enliven your faith. The practice of curiosity will be your friend in these efforts.

For example, Jennifer gained a working understanding from seminary and her ordination process of her church's beliefs and practices about the Lord's Supper. She could interpret these well enough for her congregation and for those outside her congregation who had an interest in such things, but she always wanted to know more. She dove into various books, both primary and secondary sources, and discovered that her church's thought and practice of the Sacred Meal was much richer and more interesting than anything she had experienced in a lifetime of being a part of her church. This led her to compare her church's understanding of communion with that of other church traditions and, in the process, served as kind of a second confirmation that she really belonged in the denomination of which she was a part.

Jennifer's personal study contributed to the renewal of her congregation's worship life and to a study series that later led to fresh congregational understandings of baptism, the formation and authority of Scripture, and the history of Reformed churches. The practice of curiosity by both Jennifer and her congregation resulted in living with a fresh appreciation of their own identity and mission.

Apart from some adventure in curiosity like this, Jennifer may have quickly gotten locked into a ministry-long pattern of stifling dullness and wonder-crushing anxiety. Once in those patterns it is hard for pastors to break out of them, regardless of how new or seasoned they may be.

KEY OPPORTUNITIES TO PRACTICE CURIOSITY

Curiosity about Your Next Important Learning about Yourself

New pastors often jump to their next learning about church and ministry, but I encourage you to also consider and discover what the next important learning about yourself will be. Who you are as a person will shape your ministry. At times, who you are as a person will get in the way of sustained, effective ministry. During seminary, you likely had the chance to reflect on your family of origin, your personality tendencies, and maybe even your conflict management style. What comes next?

A number of tests and surveys will lead to further reflection on who you are as a person. For example, when Jennifer took a creativity quotient test[19] it stirred her heart and mind's juices during a time when she was feeling the separation from several years of intellectual discovery and faith stretching. Most creativity quotient tests identify ways your thinking is already imaginative, inventive, and unconventional. Another positive result of these tests is that they spark curiosity, causing us to ask, "Now, why wasn't I already thinking about that? I'm obviously smart, original, and resourceful!" Even people who don't score particularly high on creative quotient tests often come away inspired to look beyond the tried and true and to rethink assumptions about the conventional.

You could choose other similar tests to stimulate and deepen your self-awareness. For example, you might learn more about your emotional intelligence, or your leadership style, or how at ease or dis-ease you are when you are alone. What makes you laugh or think or cry? What stands in the way of your playfulness? What makes you feel particularly secure and what unnerves and worries you at your core? How do you process grief and what losses linger in the shadows of your own spirit? These are areas where curiosity about yourself will raise your self-awareness and, in doing so, will allow you to enjoy more of simply being you.

Curiosity about What Your Next Joyful and Important Learning will Be about Church and Ministry

The debate about what constitutes a strong seminary curriculum continues. Some say the focus on cultivating a theological consciousness takes priority. Others contend that primary attention needs to be placed on developing pastoral imagination and skills.

19. For example, see http://www.edu-nova.com/apps/creativity.html and http://www.testmycreativity.com/.

Most schools try to balance these competing priorities, but even a school committed to equipping its students with strong pastoral leadership skills will not be able to provide its graduates with everything they need to know about renewing a congregation or managing a not-for-profit agency or engaging in deep contextual analysis and appreciation. So, then, what learning about church and ministry will you acquire as a result of your practice of curiosity?

For me, it was systems and systems thinking. My seminary's emphasis on introspection and pastoral care fostered self-awareness and calm in ministering to people in one-on-one situations, such as visiting with them in hospitals, nursing homes, and their own homes. However, I entered the first congregation I served after seminary during a time of serious conflict. I was their thirty-fourth pastor in ninety years. On an individual basis, they are some of the loveliest, kindest, committed people I know. On a congregational level in those days, though, unresolved, age-old tensions made almost any gathering of the congregation, including worship, difficult to endure. While I enjoyed positive relationships with most people in the congregation, I inevitably contributed to the systemic woes of that church due to my lack of understanding about how systems function, how they react emotionally, how they unwittingly recruit people to play certain roles, and how they tend to scapegoat truth-tellers. I spent as much time as possible during the first three years after seminary reading and participating in workshops about systems thinking and systemic dynamics.

What learning will nurture confidence in your practice of ministry? What new discovery will help you understand and enjoy being a leader in your congregation or agency? In a time when everything about church and ministry can feel new, the temptation is to batten down the hatches and brace for whatever unknown comes next. Rather than let that feeling hem you in, use it to propel you into your next learning as you practice curiosity for the sake of your calling. The discovery, energy, and wonder that you will experience in doing so will spill over into the life of the congregation.

Curiosity about an energizing interest or hobby that is not related to church and ministry

Luciana gives riding lessons to young equine lovers. Chaquetha paints landscapes. Jeff makes everything from Godly Play figures to rocking chairs in his woodworking shop. Christine loves to ride her motorcycle. Larry plays on a soccer team for people fifty years old and over on Tuesday nights. Aziz plays guitar in a coffee-shop band on Friday nights. Cindy plays doubles tennis with a clergy colleague in a nearby town who also was looking for an enjoyable and helpful release from pastoral work and congregational dynamics.

But none of these people knew how to do these things before their transition into ministry. They began their hobbies and learned their trades in their first few years after seminary. In some cases, it was a long-held dream come true. Chaquetha had wanted to paint since she was a little girl. In others, the person decided on a particular hobby after a lengthy search. That was the case with Christine, whose quest for something freeing and exciting came down to rock climbing and motorcycle riding before the latter won out.

Two factors will discourage your pursuit of a hobby during this transition. First, the inclination to over-function in the midst of your new responsibilities and others' expectations will cause you to focus more intensely on your ministry position to the neglect of other interests. Second, the many changes likely have taken sufficient emotional toll on you that you will jealously guard any free time just to decompress. This makes sense on one level, but doing so may isolate you further from intellectual and spiritual stimulation.

So what occasionally comes into your mind as a possible hobby or interest outside of ministry? Or what avocation did you put on hold during seminary that you now want to find time to pick back up again? Identify what that might be and then see yourself doing it. Let the anticipated enjoyment of the activity cultivate the needed commitment and energy to look into what it takes to get started.

Curiosity about what stifles your curiosity

This may sound like an odd practice, and you may avoid or dismiss it completely, but if you have a curiosity deficit something must be suppressing or blocking it. Brene Brown says that many of us entered into a creativity slump in late elementary school from which we have never recovered. The fear of being wrong or of being judged during those early adolescent years causes us to withdraw in self-preservation. As a result, the vulnerability needed for creativity does not occur. The creative slump can last through adulthood unless we take intentional steps to break out of the play-it-safe mentality and risk something new. Brown contends that today's innovation crisis in the United States can be traced to the creative slumps that began in childhood.[20] Let's also acknowledge that the academic and vocational pressures of seminary can contribute to and even cause a creativity slump as students seek approval from their professors and churches.

Perhaps the discomfort of being vulnerable squelches your curiosity. Or, on a related note, it's understandable during your transition into ministry that any number of responsibilities and activities will be constricted by perfectionism, a personality trait that will be exacerbated during this transition. Your fear of failure may stifle your curiosity, even though you recognize that curiosity has contributed to every success you have known in life so far. If you are the oldest child in your family of origin, you probably exercise more caution, control, and structure than others, and all these things can discourage curiosity. Or you may just be tired.

This practice seeks to awaken you to what stands in the way of being curious. You may be able to trace your lack of curiosity to an experience in your family or school or some other part of your life, but may still need professional help to identify and work

20. Brown, *Power of Vulnerability*, chapter 45.

through the barriers. Whatever time is spent on understanding and addressing your curiosity deficit is time well spent.

Curiosity in relationship to the other practices of nimbleness

In each of the "Practices" section of the chapters devoted to curiosity, clarity, agility, proximity, and temerity, I will call attention to how each practice informs and contributes to the other four practices of nimbleness, noting how each practice is strengthened by its relationship to the other four or diminished when one or more of the other four is missing.

For example, an essential dimension of clarity is the ability to become aware of the options so that they can be either ruled in or out as a possible position on an issue or course of action; so, curiosity lends a fuller menu to the possibilities for clarity. Curiosity energizes agility and leads us to experientially assess and appreciate possible paths and stances. Curiosity not only moves us into proximity to what is occurring and emerging, but it also causes us to discover more by asking penetrating questions of what is before us rather than accept default and second-hand interpretations. Finally, curiosity nurtures temerity when it not only asks why, but begins to ask why not.

Conversely, the absence of curiosity or the absence of any other practice diminishes the complementary dynamic of the five. For example, the pursuit of clarity will be stunted apart from curiosity. Agility will be less adventurous and cover less territory without curiosity. Without sufficient curiosity, we are unlikely to move beyond the familiar and the comfortable in order to get close to the action. And without curiosity, temerity is confined to what we already understand to be possible. Think about Dr. King's speech. He painted an audaciously bold picture and it started by dreaming, by imagining, by being curious about what is right, good, and possible in the lives of real people, actual communities, and concrete situation.

5

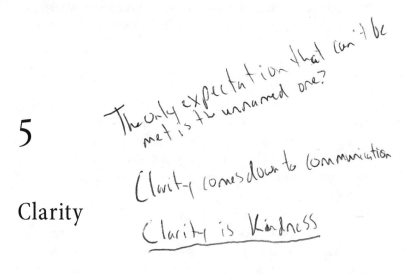

The only expectation that can't be met is the unnamed one?

Clarity comes down to communication

Clarity is Kindness

Clarity

Ambiguity: what happens in vagueness, stays in vagueness.[1]

May your life awaken
To the call of its freedom.[2]

Send us now into the world in peace, and grant us strength and courage to love and serve you with gladness and singleness of heart.[3]

Seek ye first the kingdom of God.[4]

NOAH COULDN'T MAKE SENSE of his situation. He was serving a small congregation, but he felt almost completely overwhelmed

---

1. Seen on a bumper sticker and a literary shirt. Source unknown.
2. O'Donohue, *To Bless the Space*, 30.
3. *Book of Common Prayer*, 365.
4. Matt 6:33 (KJV).

and scattered. One of his mentors suggested he place a copy of his ordination vows under the glass on his desk so that he would see what promises he had made to God and to the church about what the focus of his ministry would be. Noah read the vows almost every day at first. Later, he would notice them but often didn't take time to read them. And then at some point, that sheet of paper faded into the background, covered over with Post-it notes of calls to return, a marriage license he still needed to sign and submit to the clerk's office, a request for a reference for a parishioner's employment application, notes from the recent performance review of the custodian, and an urn of a member's ashes that somehow had fallen to him to inter in the church columbarium.

Noah was drawn to ministry because of its vocational core, that of leading worship, preaching, caring for people in distress, and shepherding the congregation toward faithful expressions of its mission, but he often felt buried beneath a barrage of tasks and duties that left him wondering almost daily exactly how tightly to draw the lines around his vocational core. Were those ordination vows just part of a ceremony? Does anybody think they really translate into ongoing leadership of a congregation or agency? Most days, Noah didn't think so.

The people of the congregation he served exacerbated this dilemma. They were so loving and supportive, but they functioned as if their primary calling was to feed enough work to their pastor to ensure that he stayed busy, regardless of whether the busy-ness connected in any way to the work of the pastor. Oblivious to the notion of a vocational core of the pastor, one might describe the demands placed on him as being captured by the title of Social Co-ordinator, Arbitrator of the Petty, and manager of a local religious franchise.[5]

One day Noah remembered how the young man at Word of Hope Church had described the situation. "The community needs a light more than ever right now and we can be that light." Noah

5. This is a frequently used comparison by Eugene Peterson, noting both that pastors are not managers and congregations are not franchises. See, for instance, *Pastor: A Memoir*, 119.

cleared the clutter of his desk and read again his ordination vows. "We're not being the light right now. In fact, my ministry is contributing to the darkness," he muttered to himself one day in his study. Instead of thinking of worship as a compelling encounter between God and God's people, he had come to view it as nothing more than a weekly task of inserting hymns and readings into a bulletin template. Instead of opening the Scriptures to allow them to breathe fresh air and new direction into the life of his congregation, just as they had breathed new life into him on so many occasions before, he now turned to the Bible begrudgingly in search of something that could lead to a sermon idea. Even his care for the congregation felt more like capitulating to manufactured dilemmas and inconsequential needs rather than helping people grow in the life and mind of Christ Jesus.

Noah decided that he would talk with the church council about why churches need pastors and why he became a pastor in the first place. He began by saying how much being a pastor still excites him, but then described how many other things he has been doing and how they have been crowding out his pastoral roles and responsibilities. He then talked about how he spends most of his time and what a betrayal of his ordination vows that feels like to him. He asked for two weeks away for a retreat to consider anew what would be at the heart of his pastoral ministry. He asked the church council to think about what the priorities for their pastor should be in light of their own mission statement.

Almost immediately, a woman said, "We do this every time. We throw all this work on the pastor that we should be doing. The pastor gets completely worn down and then thinks the only option is to move to another church. We've got to change the way we do things if we expect a different result." Noah and the congregation negotiated several points of concern over the next several months and they continue to thrive together today, eight years after he first arrived at that church.

This process began because Noah took the initiative to talk with the church council. It took a lot to risk that conversation, including the willingness to be helped, which not every pastor has.

In the end, the conversation put both Noah and the congregation on a new path together.

CLARITY AS A PRACTICE

For several summers, I was a regular guest speaker at a Jewish summer camp for high-school-age youth. The rabbis and other camp leaders wanted the campers to encounter people of different faiths and to engage in a thoughtful conversation with their guests about their tradition's beliefs, commitments and practices. According to the camp counselors, the teenagers held distorted opinions of Christians as a result of listening to particularly shrill voices from the Christian community. They had not heard the Christian faith discussed openly, sensitively, or thoughtfully by someone from a more mainstream perspective.

It would worry some people that I was Christianity's representative to those sixty or so Jewish teenagers. I can only hope that they gained as much as I did from those conversations. You see, I grew up in the church, and over the years I have breathed so much church air that at times I have nearly asphyxiated myself on church acronyms, Christian slogans, and a whole array of unhelpful shorthand for Scripture and hymns. All that goes out the window when a young Jewish woman five feet away asks in the company of her peers, "Do you believe that Jesus was different from Moses or Isaiah and, if so, how and why?" Or, "Aren't all Christian holidays a baptized version of Jewish ones?" Or, "Do you really believe in that hocus-pocus of bread becoming the body of Jesus just because someone says certain words over it?" At that point, there is no place to hide.

Much of Eurocentric Christianity, which includes traditionally mainline denominations in the United States, either devolves into an uncritical personal piety that asks its adherents to forget much of what they know about their world, or a socially conscious expression of faith that doesn't expect its adherents to ground their activism in Scripture, theology, and the history of the church. It's hard for the people in the first group to defend their positions apart from a circular argument, and is equally difficult for people in the second group to rule out any position of faith as long as it is sincerely held.

Neither of these positions is very helpful. Clarity doesn't result from reducing everything in an attempt to eliminate ambiguity. Rather, clarity emerges as we understand how the key parts of our theological worldview and gospel priorities translate into our lives of faith and practice of ministry.

There's nothing like our own life of worship and faith to provide this clarity. Calvin described the church as a "Christian sanctuary functioning as a schoolhouse, a place of concentration, focus and learning—and ultimately a place where the catechism and especially the Bible may be engaged and internalized such that they form how disciples experience and live in the wider world."[6] That internalization happens both for the pastor and the congregation through steady, creative, and bold engagement with the theological threads. Liturgy, says Jonathan Z. Smith, "serves as a kind of focusing lens for human practitioners in their intellectual, moral, and other formation. A sacred place is a place of clarification."[7]

The value of clarity is highlighted in many fields. For example, Ronald Heifetz claims that most organizational challenges can be traced to one of four types.[8] One of those is vagueness and confusion about the gap between the stated values of organizations and the way those organizations use their time and allocate their resources. New pastors can fall prey to a similar pattern. The piercing clarity needed for your congregation or agency to engage in a joyfully impactful season of ministry turns, in large part, on your capacity to think and act with greater focus and specificity. Otherwise, the extraneous—that which falls beyond your vocational core—will consume your thoughts and energy and lead

6. Boulton, *Life in God*, 102.

7. Smith, "Bare Facts of Ritual," 53–65.

8. Heifetz et al., *Practice of Adaptive Leadership*, 72–99. The four archetypes posited by Heifetz and his colleagues are 1) a gap between espoused values and behavior, 2) competing commitments, 3) speaking the unspeakable, and 4) work avoidance.

you to operate outside your calling as a pastor and your purpose for being with this particular community at this particular time. General goodwill, as pleasant and helpful as it often is, will not renew a community, and it alone will not support you through this transition. Vagueness is the enemy. It is the enemy to a life-giving faith. It is the enemy to the mission of the church. And it is the enemy to your transition into ministry.

On the other hand, piercing clarity about your understanding of the gospel and the particular work to which you have been called fosters an expression of faith and leadership from which both you and others will benefit. Very few have this level of clarity when they graduate from seminary, but hopefully your seminary experience gave you a taste of that clarity and sufficient tools and encouragement to continue to develop it throughout your ministry.

You, no doubt, are encountering concreteness and particularities in your transition into ministry in ways you did not during seminary. There's nothing abstract or theoretical about where you are serving. Multiple variables from the lives of real people and the community have entered into your ministry situation and demand your attention and appreciation. It's time to bring your theological clarity from seminary and the particularities of your ministry setting into conversation with each other. Theological, contextual clarity involves holding themes and practices up to the light of the Christian story, honing in on what gives life, and then embodying and articulating that life-giving faith in the midst of a people.

KEY OPPORTUNITIES TO PRACTICE CLARITY

Clarity about why you are in this place, in this moment, with this community.

Each beginning of a new ministry provides its own context. Every season of a church, agency, and wider community brings its own opportunities and challenges. Admittedly, some of these represent ongoing opportunities and challenges whose work stretches beyond several seasons. Others are left over from when people didn't notice them, or ignored them, or never adequately addressed them. Unfinished business is a part of life and a big part of ministry, but during this transition, for clarity's sake, you still ask this question: what hopeful, imaginative work falls to us in this particular window of time? To what is God calling us by bringing us together? At its best, this practice yields piercing clarity to that question.

A pastor once said to me, "I believe my congregation is pregnant. I'm not sure what we are about to give birth to, but we are convinced at our church that something good is on its way." More than maintaining the status quo, or fretting over the various deficits you are becoming aware of, or only spending time trying to fix broken programs and processes, where do you perceive life waiting to be born? If you guide the probe gently over the belly of your congregation or agency, where do you hear the strongest heartbeat, and how can you midwife this possibility to life?

Perhaps you will help facilitate long-needed healing and focus within the congregation or agency that you serve. Or the new life may come from more intentional engagement with the immediate community that you can model and lead. Or you may midwife a demonstrably deeper faith through your preaching, teaching, and leading of worship. Or might your pregnant congregation or agency be on the cusp of giving birth to a more lively, intergenerational community? This may finally be the season when your congregation or agency renews its organizational life so that it supports mission instead of draining resources away from it.

You may get an idea during the interview or appointment process about what work will fall to you in this particular place and in this particular window of time, but it's more likely that this picture will develop for you over several months or even the first couple of years. Still, be attentive during the early months of your transition into ministry and enjoy the attention the congregation or agency is giving you. You both will carry the sense of being pregnant. You'll believe something good is ahead. Take note of what you hear, see, read, and observe. Look for clues everywhere for what longs to be born in this season. The more you are able to discern, recognize, and claim the new life that this particular season can bring, the greater the joy at its birth and the greater fulfillment for you in your role as a midwife.

Clarity about the use of time and passion in approaching this season's work.

Time is required to do any of the things described in the first practice above. No congregation or agency experiences renewal as a result of a single act, just as no one achieves a level of expertise apart from extensive, sustained practice. Malcolm Gladwell gives several examples in his book *The Tipping Point* of professionals who arrive at a level of accomplishment and effectiveness only after ten thousand hours of intentional practice.[9] Organizations (especially voluntary, religious ones) do not develop a life-giving, missionally-focused rhythm in less time than that. You are just beginning your ten thousand hours of practice, which is why I believe the transition into ministry is a five-to-seven-year process.

Because of the very real challenges of this transition, new pastors often feel like time has collapsed on them as they find themselves obsessing about their next six months of ministry. Time is the gift that allows you to stretch out the vision of the ministry into which you will live and serve. Your transition into ministry will benefit from taking the long view. In fact, the long view is necessary. It will be the gentle pull that helps you move with increasing confidence from one season to the next. A sustained, reflective, undivided engagement with congregational life and ministry is critical to the formation of pastoral identity and skill. The more time and passion you devote to a specific challenge, the more quickly you will begin to exercise agency in all areas of your calling, including your transition into ministry.

But time is not the only ingredient of this practice. With what commitment and passion will you give yourself over to the particular work of this season together? With what clarity and passion will you address those things which, in the gospel's view and

9. Gladwell, *Outliers*, 41.

in your own heart, cannot stand? As Bono puts it, how will you betray the age?[10] Drawing on Brendan Kennelly's poem "Book of Judas," Bono contends that every age has its conceits, foibles, and moral blind spots. About which ones will you get specific in your teaching, leading, and advocacy?

How might I betray the age?

Bono cites slavery as an obvious blind spot of a particular age, noting that only a few civic and religious leaders betrayed the age and challenged that atrocity. Hopefully, you started becoming familiar with some of the opportunities for ministry during the search or appointment process that brought you to this place. A physician friend of mine says, "Doctors change lives. That's what we do." With God's help and the community's gifts, what part of life will you attempt to change for the sake of a fairer and more tender world? What is worth betraying the age by spending part of your transition into ministry? On what passion, value, and commitment will you draw to address that issue? What gifts and skills will you develop and employ toward this effort?

Clarity about what your guard rails will be and how they will function for you.

As you arrive at clarity about what this particular season of ministry holds (the first practice of clarity) and begin to bring to bear your passion and commitment to those opportunities and challenges (the second practice), you will be tempted frequently to fragment your focus and spend your time in other ways. Members of your faith community nervous about change will encourage you to look away at times. You may become impatient at the pace of change and allow your thoughts and interests to drift elsewhere. Conflict and controversy may threaten to derail your ministry. In the most extreme cases, new pastors have engaged in self-destructive behavior that has resulted in an early exit from ministry.

Organizational theories often use the term "guardrails" to describe what will keep us focused on our mission. You will find

10. Bono, "Because We Can, We Must," paras. 12–16.

the term useful for your transition into ministry. You want to be reminded that this work matters to much to you to lose track of how you are spending your time. The emotional demands of the transition into ministry are such that maintaining interest and focus in your pastoral work can be daunting, so you want alarms to go off at the first sign of losing those things. That won't spell the end of your ministry. Pastors of every age and years of experience struggle with this at some point and to some degree, but you are new to this. You are finding your voice and rhythm. The guardrails will help you know and be honest about needed areas of growth.

These days, says Andrew Sullivan, the greater threat is not hedonism, but distraction. Though not the only source of it, technology—with its mindless web-surfing and the emotional neediness of constant social media contact—can cause us to lose the focus of our ministry and drain hours from our weeks.[11] More than just your pastoral leadership suffers when this happens. The energy and emotional engagement necessary to keep moving in your transition into ministry will drift as well, and the motivation for an already difficult process will stall.

Pastoral ministry is a juggling act. We arrive at clarity over time by deciding not just which balls we will keep in the air, but which ones we will let drop. Saying yes only means something when we have said no to some things. And in doing so, don't assume that you have either delighted or disappointed someone in the church as a result of what you have said yes or no to. Rather, base your decision on your guardrails. If you are ordained, your ordination vows provide guardrails. If you are not ordained, your employment agreement and job description offer a similar kind of guidance. This doesn't mean you'll never do anything not mentioned in your ordination vows or job description, but it does mean that you will pay unrelenting and unapologetic attention to that which forms your vocational core.

Which balls are plastic?
Which balls are glass? Let your yes be yes
& your no be no.
How do we balance our guardrails
with the guardrails of others &
the congregation as a whole?

11. Sullivan, "Human Being."

Clarity about whether your time allocation supports the priorities of your vocational core.

What would be revealed by a biopsy of your calendar? Would the priorities established by the previous practice be supported by the amount of time allocated to each one? Perhaps we all need a nimbleness Fitbit, one that would only measure the steps we have taken in the direction of our values, priorities, and goals.

We all experience some disparity between our espoused priorities and our enacted ones. In ministry, some weeks will be so severely skewed because of the unusual or unexpected that they simply have to be thrown out rather than averaged into your time allocation. Most weeks, however, the week will appear before you as a more or less clean slate, waiting on you to decide how to spend it.[12] The inclination of new pastors to over-function, often in an attempt to prove themselves and to please others, can sabotage the best of efforts at allocating time according to priorities. And because so many congregations and agencies perpetually live in the reactive mode, they reward their pastors and directors for being equally reactive and distracted, even if that reactivity consistently undermines the long-term vitality of the congregation or agency.

In the earlier days of personal computing, it wasn't unusual to find that we could only have so many windows open at a time. Even now, with nearly unimaginable technological advances, there's a limit to how many windows can be open at one time. Our laptop's RAM will determine that. The temptation, especially during the transition into ministry, is to open as many windows as possible and then exhaust yourself from trying to keep them open. For example, in addition to working in the windows of leading worship, interpreting the faith; caring for parishioners; guiding the mission of the congregation or agency; and spending quality, renewing time with your loved ones, you are participating in a project with the women's group, serving on the board of one community

12. Admittedly, this is truer of pastors of congregations than agency directors, but agency directors also can slip into the reactive mode to the point that they no longer take time for visioning and long-term strategy.

service club and participating in two others, coordinating a school festival, and organizing special services that will be hosted by the ministerial association. And in many cases, these ventures represent the more reasonable causes in which one might participate. You also may find yourself washing dishes, emptying trash cans, restarting the pilot light on the furnace, and shoveling snow.

I once spent three whole days helping two other people rewire the church for the new sound system. I am not above doing any of these things, and I trust that you aren't either, but I have wondered often what the impact might have been if I had spent the same three days planning creative worship, preparing an inspiring sermon series, and imagining how our congregation might be a source of uplift and support to the broader community. Perhaps I was looking for a distraction. Maybe I wasn't excited to be a pastor that week. What is clear is that my time allocation did not represent the commitments I made—the commitments that the church asked me to make—in my ordination vows.

Clarity in relationship to the other practices of nimbleness.

Clarity strengthens the other four practices so that your life and ministry express a focus and shape that is recognizable to others and life-giving to yourself. For example, clarity brings into focus the blurred edges of curiosity, sharpening it so that what is being considered can be explored, expressed, and addressed well. Clarity guides agility toward the intended aim, making agility less haphazard, reactive, and random. Clarity causes you to identify what is emerging so that you can get close to it, then helps you see the rough boundaries of what is emerging so you can handle it with care and impact. And finally, clarity leads to temerity. (We'll also say later that temerity leads to clarity, which is true.) Clarity involves risk as you choose particular paths, make specific commitments, and articulate unambiguous positions, all the while not choosing other paths, commitments, or positions. Those choices and commitments will determine the extent to which you claim for yourself a focused, fulfilling, and fierce ministry.

Clarity, on the other hand, is frayed and undermined by the absence of a vigorous curiosity. There's simply not enough input of imaginative ideas and compelling possibilities for clarity to emerge. At the same time, without agility, then clarity becomes an intellectual exercise that fails to gain traction on anything that matters. Without proximity, clarity will be stifled because you will not be close enough to the opportunity or challenge to give it definition. As we have noted already, temerity does not take root and grow in vague soil. Clarity provides the environment needed for temerity's commitments and convictions to take on clear and adventurous expression.

6

Agility

The trick to Jazz improvisation is playing music with both spontaneous creativity and intentional conviction.[1]

The one who knows one language knows none.[2]

Christ calls us now, as long ago beside the Galilee
The call went to common folk, "Come now; come follow me!"
So when we hear, respond, and go, We too must leave behind
The trappings and encumbrances Possessing life and mind.[3]

JENNIFER KNEW CHURCH SYSTEMS move slowly. She had sat through enough committee meetings and task forces before going to seminary to not be shocked by the intransigence of congregational processes, but she experienced those challenges differently

1. Source unknown. Quoted in "Jazz Improvisation," para. 1.
2. Goethe, *Maxims and Reflections*, 13.
3. "Christ Calls Us Now, As Long Ago," in Huber, *Singing Faith*, 29.

when it was her pastoral agenda encountering one roadblock after another. A simple proposal to connect congregational leaders with neighborhood association leaders was met with paralyzing indecision. Later, during her first year at Grace Church, Jennifer announced that she would be attending a local housing summit that would feature a conversation between the emergency housing shelters in the city and those agencies that were more focused on home ownership for the economically marginalized. She thought it provided an opportunity to understand the larger housing issues better and to contribute to an important conversation, but members of her church council declined to attend because they feared the summit would be contentious and divisive.

The exasperatingly slow pace with which her congregation acted on things caused Jennifer to rather quickly become convinced that she could best effect change in the world through avenues other than the church. She lived almost daily with this tension between wanting to be a pastor and enjoying pastoral work, on the one hand, and desiring to exercise a positive impact on situations that cried out for hope and healing on the other.

So, despite her frustration, she sought ways to balance her desire to continue as a pastor with opportunities in the community that would make a difference. When she advocated with two other women in the community for transitional housing, which the summit revealed was really the missing piece in the housing equation, she realized that the city council and the local agencies moved nearly as slowly and cautiously as her congregation. It was clear that very little financial support was earmarked for this effort. However, she articulated the need for transitional housing so compellingly that a strong coalition of people, networks, and resources came together, and within eighteen months, four transitional homes were established. That coalition consisted of concerned individuals, local landlords, the city housing agency, a fraternity from the local college, and faith communities from four different religious traditions.

Jennifer's congregation still rehashed old things too often and reacted defensively at new ideas, but the transitional housing initiative seemed to nurture a little more clarity and decisiveness about its mission. Jennifer still questioned whether the church could be a trusted partner and a reliable participant in God's transforming of the world, but the burden of the earlier tension eased. And just as important, the more she and her congregation and the housing coalition navigated opportunities and challenges, the more agile she became as a pastor and community leader. Her agile engagement with this and other issues helped her appreciate the challenges that churches and communities face when change and transition are at hand. At the same time, that engagement contributed to her understanding of her own transition into ministry and highlighted the importance of her continued movement forward in that transition.

AGILITY AS A PRACTICE

In previous chapters, we have described some things about the contemporary landscape for ministry in the United States. The question is not whether church decline is taking place. Every study reports losses for church bodies in the United States. It doesn't matter whether they have a denominational affiliation or self-describe as non-denominational. Liberal or conservative, historic or contemporary, urban or rural—the losses are real. Some are losing participants at a much slower rate, but still losing.

The question usually gets framed—and rather desperately, at that—as this: "What can we do as the church about the losses of members, money, and influence?" I want to reframe the question and ask this instead: "As followers of Jesus and as pastors, what matters most to us, and how will we express those values and commitments in our ministry?" Wouldn't it be regrettable to be sucked into the black hole of a narrative of decline and anxiety, and to miss opportunities to impact positively individuals and communities as a result?

I know some people see the pastoral life as a ticket to a certain level of acceptance, security, and recognition. Those aren't bad things, unless they get in the way of embodying our values and commitments and become barriers to engaging opportunities and challenges that call to us. In some cases, perhaps an argument can be made to channel every possible resource toward keeping the doors of a church open for a small group of longtime members, but we have to question that strategy if propping up a congregation takes resources away from the hurting neighbors in our midst. Ironically, just as Jesus promised, pastors and congregations that give themselves away for the sake of the world often discover a whole new future for themselves.

Ministry will not be like seminary. You can't spend days and days writing an exegesis paper, but neither can you leave behind the theological consciousness and the value clarification that come from seminary studies. Continue to enrich your life and ministry with the study patterns (or even better ones!) that you practiced in seminary, but also know that ministry is not a sedentary vocation by its nature. Jesus constantly moved from one situation to another, including moving in and out of prayer times. Jesus' disciples were sent to engage people and circumstances. We, too, are sent. It's just that once we get there—wherever "there" may be—we tend to react, at best, and sometimes withdraw completely. Just as we talked about in the chapter on the practice of clarity, the result is that we get disconnected from the calling that energizes us and distanced from the concerns that first claimed us for this work.

Pastors generally aren't known as agile creatures. Nor are congregations, which are built for stability and perpetuation, not for innovation and adventure. As a ministry colleague once phrased it to me, "We are trying to think outside the box with the people who built the box!" When we remember that, we shouldn't be too surprised with the stubbornness people exhibit toward certain ideas and traditions. (We also should keep before us that pastors exhibit a similar kind of recalcitrance as everyone else.) To congregants, the church is an anchor in the most positive sense. To consider changing its priorities and rituals is to tinker with the sacred. At the same time, you are holding certain things sacred during your transition into ministry because that is the way we survive change and complete transitions.

On a recent mission trip to rehab houses in an underserved area, thirty teenagers slept at a nearby church. On their first night there, a member of the church strolled into fellowship hall, made his way to a telephone that hung on the wall, and posted a sign that read "No Long Distance Calls." It was an act of stewardship, I'm sure, but in the time it took this man to post that cardboard sign and walk out, half of the youth had already taken a picture of the man and the sign with their smartphones and posted the picture online so that family and friends around the world could see it. Within seconds, all kinds of people were seeing the same sign. That's what half the youth group did. You could hear the other half of the group asking, "What's a long distance call?"

I don't know what parallel you will find in your first ministry position, but it's likely that some similar relic will be trotted out and honored. Show some humility and sensitivity when that occurs, because chances are that you are holding keepsakes of another time and place in your heart as you seek to navigate your transition into ministry. Don't let your impatience with yourself during the challenges of your transition into ministry spill over into impatience with those around you.

The good news is that not all congregations and agencies are confounded and hemmed in by organizational obsessions and institutional timidity. The church is a sign of God's realm in our midst.[4] The church prays at least weekly "Thy kingdom come."[5] Some pastors and faith communities put themselves on the line every day, identifying opportunities, thinking creatively, and acting courageously. Their calling will not allow them to sit on the sidelines. Righteous indignation, or what some more recently coined as holy discontent,[6] rises within individuals and communities that announces that "This injustice cannot stand." A sense of urgency stirs within us. Opportunities excite us. We are outraged by senseless acts of violence, by children going hungry, and

---

4. Eph 3:10.

5. Matt 6:10.

6. See Hybels, *Holy Discontent*.

by whole communities being abandoned by city and commercial planners.

But the engagement is often tepid, at best. Instead of leading, we allow the policies and processes put in place for stability's sake to go unquestioned, bogging down our progress on mission and impact. We also get very timid around the possibility of mistakes and failures. Organizations and institutions do this pretty consistently. New pastors find this to be particularly challenging, especially during the transition into ministry when they likely are over-functioning to begin with. The understandable desire to do everything just right can lead to a pattern of ministry that seeks to protect pastors from failure and criticism rather than deploy pastors in the fulfilling work of congregational leadership and community transformation.

At this point, you will find that the road forks in the subtlest of ways. Each fork offers its own rewards. It reminds me of the way God framed the situation for the Israelites: "I call heaven and earth to witness against you today that I have set before you life and death, blessings and curses. Choose life so that you and your descendants may live."[7] It's a beautiful promise, but its possibilities and challenges, like the fork in the road, come to us in whispers, nudges, and light knocks on the door. In the letters between Boris Pasternak and Olga Ivinskaya, there is the following beautiful recognition: "When a great moment knocks on the door of your life, its sound is often no louder than the beating of your heart and it is very easy to miss it."[8]

One path is to pour yourself into institutional maintenance. Doing so promises much affirmation, and maybe even a few material rewards. Congregants and agency volunteers will appreciate all the attention you are giving them, even if most of what you are doing further guarantees the decline of the congregation or agency. The people likely will experience your leadership as nostalgically calming as you convene meetings to discuss ministry initiatives that should have died decades ago. They will appreciate

7. Deut 30:19.
8. O'Donohue, *To Bless the Space*, 4.

your interest in their personal and institutional stories. They also will breathe a sigh of relief at the way your slow-moving approach seems to diffuse heated arguments and divisive conflicts.

This approach will suit you well as one who is moving from the familiarity of seminary into the often ambiguous waters of a new ministry. Enough change is occurring in your life that you will want nothing more than a couple of quiet years to help you make sense of a new place and to give you the space to begin the emotional, spiritual adjustment of this transition. Along with increasing your salary whenever possible from being so understanding and well-liked, the people's support will feel like a security blanket during your transition.

But there can be something seductive about this approach. We can pay too much attention to the congregation's longing for comfort or to the agency's desire for harmony and miss opportunities to strengthen the ministry and bless the community of which the congregation or agency is a part. In the process, the practice of agility that is key to your transition into ministry gets squelched, and the inward focus that has plagued your organization begins to hamper your transition into ministry. Like Jesus said to Peter on the resurrection lakeshore, "someone else will fasten a belt around you and take you where do not wish to go."[9] You end up devoting yourself to values of survival and to commitments of not rocking the boat, which means that the holy discontent of your calling gets set aside.

What changes if we return not just to our calling, but to the Caller? Agility is born from a God who delights in fresh expressions of shalom and well-being. Sometimes that is an entirely new thing, as in Isaiah: "Do not remember the former things, or consider the things of old. I am about to do a new thing; now it springs forth, do you not perceive it? I will make a way in the wilderness and rivers in the desert."[10] At other times, God renews what is already present: "See, I am making all things new."[11] Our agility is our participation

9. John 21:18.
10. Isa 43:18–19.
11. Rev 21:5a.

in the new thing God is doing in our midst. Perhaps in your congregation or agency, that will be a totally new, adventurous thing to which God is calling you. In other cases, it may be the vigorous renewal of an initiative or situation that has suffered decline and irrelevance for too long. Your agile participation in the new thing God is doing will keep you moving through your transition into ministry by keeping you connected to your call to ministry and by providing a helpful perspective to the intransigence you may be encountering in your congregation or agency.

Organizational intransigence is not the only situation that calls out for pastoral agility today and it's definitely not the most interesting one. For example, consider the theological agility required to live and serve well in a richly pluralistic world. People are asking questions such as these: how many paths are there to God, and are all of them equally valid? Who can and cannot be married? How can people be both spiritual and religious? What will the changes in our town or neighborhood mean for our church, and will we help reshape the new community or just bemoan the losses? What new learning can occur with worldwide opportunities for access and collaboration? Why is the church declining in this country, while at the same time some of our most cherished ideas are gaining prominence?

These questions pulse through the church and society every day. They call for remarkable personal, pastoral, and theological agility. Pastoral agility means being grounded in the Christian story, yet conversant with a wide range of voices, and able to move nimbly and helpfully between the important congregational and community conversations that are going on at any given moment. This level of theological reflection and practice creates space for congregations and agencies to draw vividly and deeply on the sources of Christian heritage and recognize the contributions they make to current topics and circumstances. For example, we seem so impoverished every time the United States considers or engages in military action, as if we are at a total loss for how we might gauge the appropriateness of preemptive action or aggressive retaliation. And yet, Christians have been theologically reflecting on this since at least the fourth century, when Augustine addressed the matter. Scripture, of course, addresses the issue even earlier.

Again, the road forks. One temptation will be to disappear emotionally (and maybe even physically) when such conversations arise. Doing so will impede your transition into ministry considerably. Engaging these interesting and life-giving questions of faith, on the other hand, will stir the same vocational impulses within you that first caused you to consider ministry as a fulfilling, exciting expression of your values and commitments. Nothing could be more helpful as you navigate your transition into ministry.

Another opportunity for theological agility emerges with the topic of leanness. In the American culture, the word "small" means inadequate and irrelevant. A lack of resources sends people scurrying into narratives other than our life-giving faith story. Scarcity worries us, especially and ironically those of us who have the most resources. We are taught always to want more. This has happened all too often as the church in this country has declined in numbers and influence. We can wring our hands in anxiety, which many do, or we can ask whether we have allowed our cultural biases to override our theological imagination.

In Scripture, leanness is not only celebrated, but is prescribed. Ezekiel is told by the LORD to pack an exile's bag, which meant he would only take with him what he could fit through a hole in the wall.[12] Jesus sent the disciples to do their work with very few trappings—no purse, no bag, and no sandals.[13] And while we want to be careful not to celebrate the suffering of poverty, Jesus called to the attention of the disciples a widow who put into the treasury two copper coins.[14] I often thought of the last congregation that I served as a widow church. We didn't have the most up-to-date building, elaborate programming, or expansive financial resources. Over time, I came to be rather thankful about the situation. Had we possessed those things, they almost certainly would have gotten in the way of making important theological commitments

12. Ezek 12:1–7.

13. Luke 10:4.

14. Mark 12:41–44.

about being a welcoming congregation of radical and generous hospitality. In other words, the material resources would have seriously hampered the agility we needed to live into our calling as a congregation.

Agility doesn't mean constantly overreacting to opportunities and trying to make things happen at a moment's notice. Not everything that comes along will match your calling and mission. Rather, agility depends on clarity in order to know what opportunities to seize and which ones to let pass by. But when it is clear that an opportunity that falls clearly within your pastoral and congregational vocation has presented itself, agility allows for a responsiveness to the opportunity. The congregation is ready to take hold of opportunities when they come its way, even if the leaders aren't completely sure what the next several steps may be in living into that particular ministry.

Agility absolutely cannot mean shady and shifty. The quality of relationships nurtured over time prepare people to respond well and quickly when an opportunity to bless the community presents itself. It's true that most people are tired of wasting their time. They want to use their gifts and resources to ease the pain of the world, but agility can only kick in if the groundwork of reliable relationships has been accomplished. Pastors who aren't trusted will not be given the informal authority to lead. Pastors who cannot trust others to engage in nimble ministry can be likened to helicopter parents who hover over their children. We need empowering, encouraging leaders, not helicopter pastors.

KEY OPPORTUNITIES TO PRACTICE AGILITY

Develop Relational Agility

You will encounter unbelievably fascinating people in your ministry. I hesitate even to suggest categories because they almost certainly will defy definition and classification. They will surprise you with their interests and their closely held secrets. Their stories will make you laugh, cry, and ask for more. What keeps them up at night will amaze you. Of course, the very things that will bring you delight also will frustrate you. (Just a reminder here that the people with whom you journey likely will experience you as both fascinating and frustrating.) Such is the nature of relationships. They make things possible in many cases. In others, however, distrust, suspicion, and narrowness get in the way as people overthink how others in the room will respond to thoughts, ideas, and plans. In other words, people don't always trust that their relationships can hold the honesty and passion needed for important conversations. There's always far more going on in a meeting of people than meets the eye.

Part of the intransigence of congregations and agencies is that most meeting rooms simply aren't big enough to hold the emotional impulses and the deeply held passions of even a small group of people.

Relational agility is a key practice for the transition into ministry. You will be juggling your own deeply held commitments in the midst of emotional upheaval and numerous changes. Your reflection on your own story can help you listen more closely to the stories of others. At the same time, as you listen attentively and pastorally to the stories of those in your congregation or agency, you will hear resonant themes and examples of change and transition. Allow the shared life and the exchange of stories to bolster your clarity about yourself and your ministry. This will help you overcome the common occurrence of the system distorting your mood and priorities.

An Anglican nun named Margaret Magdalen comments on the pain and suffering Jesus encountered in his ministry. The way he dealt with it, says Magdalen, is the difference between a vacuum cleaner and a dishwasher. "The vacuum cleaner sucks up all the dirt and keeps it in the bag; whereas the dishwasher cleans up the dirty dishes and immediately spews forth all the filth into the drains."[15] Obviously, one allows for a lot more relational agility. It is difficult to be fully present to the person in front of you if you are still emotionally connected to the last person you encountered. This doesn't

15. Tutu, *God Has A Dream*, 285.

mean that you stop caring about people as soon as you leave their sight, but rather that you are cultivating enough relational agility to enter into new situations with people with the same devoted and unencumbered care as you demonstrated before.

Few things undercut agility, as well as the other practices of nimbleness, like depression. Unfortunately, depression is a common malady among those in ministry, and it can be especially challenging during the transition into ministry. If you ever suspect that you are becoming depressed, seek help immediately and often. Do this, first, for the sake of your own well-being, then for the sake of those in your family, and then for the sake of your ministry.

Develop a Repertoire of Leadership Strategies

Successful sports teams often are said to have more than one game. In basketball, for instance, this might mean that the team makes difficult shots from the perimeter as well as navigates well closer to the basket. In football, this usually means that an offensive team can catch its opponent off guard because it can run and pass the ball equally well. In baseball, it even applies to individual players. A pitcher, for example, needs to be able to throw several different kinds of pitches—a fastball, a breaking pitch, a slider, and a change-up. As Goethe said, if you only know one language you don't know any.[16]

When it comes to how pastors think about building on congregational and agency strengths and effecting important, timely change, they need more than one game. The transition into ministry provides a great time to explore and nurture a repertoire of leadership strategies. The learning that will result from this exploration will benefit you across many seasons, of course, but during this particular season this practice will keep you engaged and enlivened about the work you are doing.

Over time, you will come to resist consistently the notion that as a pastor you have to respond to every person and situation

16. Goethe, *Maxims and Reflections.*

the same way. You will want (and need) to respond pastorally and professionally, but that doesn't mean you will respond to four different church members in exactly the same fashion any more than you would respond to your four children with exactly the same approach and spirit.

Israel Galindo recommends making regular assessments about our repertoire of responses to people and situations by asking, "Do [you] have a wider range of responsive options than you did previously? Can you both act differently and think divergently?"[17] Do you hear the proactive intentionality in those questions? New pastors often feel off-balance, which is a terribly vulnerable feeling when people can and will say almost anything in the world to their pastor without the slightest notice or regret. Even as you are finding your own balance as a person and pastor, the transition into ministry provides space to begin developing a repertoire of responsiveness. With some people, you will respond every time with tenderness and a double portion of listening. Some situations will be ripe for appropriate and well-timed humor. Still others will cry out for a clear and prophetic word.

Hopefully, not all of your ministry will be spent reacting and responding. You will be positioned to initiate and lead change and those things require agility and a repertoire of strategies. In some cases, an appreciative inquiry approach will help surface latent gifts. In other cases, a critical analysis of the ministries and processes in place will be a beneficial starting point. Leading change means articulating a vision of where the congregation or agency is going, but it also involves helping people let go—or at least loosen their grip—on cherished things of the past. Depending on the circumstances, you may be the champion of a cause or you may empower others who will champion the cause. You may knock down whatever barriers are in the way of fulfilling the mission or you may function as a set of guardrails to say what falls within the mission and what does not.

Most processes, whether you are responding or taking the lead, will be messy. This will add to the messiness of your transition

17. Galindo, "Six 'Tells,'" para. 6.

into ministry, but this practice also will serve to keep you moving through the transition. The more you learn about various leadership strategies, the more you will engage them. The more you engage them, the more comfortable you will feel in your new role and the more in control of your own transition you will be.

Practicing Agility in Lean Situations

It is beyond dispute that we will be doing ministry in an environment where the resources and partnerships must be cultivated afresh. That's not to say that resources and partnerships are completely gone. That would be the sad, old narrative of decline, and it's just not true. The reality is that, outside of a few well-endowed congregations and agencies, we will be doing ministry at the same time that we are cultivating generosity, developing partnerships, and looking under every bush and behind every door for resources.

This adds a layer of challenge on you right now because you are probably already feeling a little lean during your transition into ministry. You are being pulled in several different directions as you learn a new place and a new leadership role, all the while making sure that you and your family are taking the necessary and hopefully enjoyable steps toward settling in. Resentment can build as you attempt to balance the personal emotions of change and new pastoral responsibilities. Many days you'll experience that balancing act as trying to reconcile two competing loyalties, and it will seem like you are failing at both of them because you feel unsatisfied with the care you are giving yourself and inadequate for the ministry to which you have been called. This practice is intended to help with this quandary.

Three to four times a week, do something outside church and ministry that involves very little resources. Doodle for an hour. Build something from scraps of material around your home. Visit an area of the community that consistently performs well with inadequate resources.

Then, after detaching long enough to settle your spirit, brainstorm an idea that would bless the community and block out from your mind all thoughts of what it might cost. Draw stick figures of the partners you will need for this idea to become a reality. Relax for another hour and think who those stick figures might represent in your community. Eventually start the ministry with what Eric Reis calls the minimal viable product (MVP), which is to begin it with what is minimally necessary.[18] Don't ask whether this will succeed or if it will last for ten or twenty years. Ignore the uncertainty of it. Just get it going. Experiment with it. Allow it to fail if it needs to. Sit back and think about what you have just done. Consider what you have learned from it. Imagine telling a few people at your church or agency. Then forget about it for a while. Repeat.

Pivoting toward Opportunities

Have you ever played a video game and watched a figure hit the boundary over and over without ever turning around and going in a different direction? What's missing in this case is the ability to pivot and go in a new direction. The practice of pivoting during the transition into ministry, like the other practices, will enhance both your practice of ministry and your emotional, spiritual well-being, but it won't be easy. Congregations and agencies become accustomed to banging into the same dead-end boundary over and over again.

Agility in church and community leadership compares favorably to soccer. If you take a direct angle toward the ball, by the time you get there you will have missed the action. It will have moved on to somewhere else. So the effective practice of agility calls for anticipation of where the action is about to go next and the willingness, ability, and nerve to pivot in that direction. And sometimes the pivot doesn't lead us directly into intense action, but rather into a clearing, an open field, where we can evaluate things from a less attached perspective.

Let me share an example from my own ministry. For eleven years I served a wonderful congregation on the edge of a major

18. Reis, *Lean Start-Up*, 77.

college campus. The campus expanded every year to where it nearly grew around the church. Congregational leaders and I had been told by denominational leaders and numerous consultants that focusing on college students was not a good use of our time and resources. They even cited a strong congregation down the street that had poured hundreds of thousands of dollars into staff and programming for a college-age ministry only to achieve very meager and erratic results, but a few of us just couldn't let go of this idea, not with the college practically at our door.

So one year, as students were arriving for the fall semester, we decided to go all out to welcome students not just to campus, but to our church. We did a lot of advertising, made a lot of personal connections, and planned a great initial event. We weren't sure what we would do if more than two hundred college students showed up, but we would make something good happen. As it turns out, that wasn't our challenge. One student from the college showed up and he had actually grown up in our congregation! It was a total flop. Or maybe it was among the most important learnings we had during those years. Either way, we pivoted and never said another word about it, other than naming some learnings. Later, when we were living into our more natural gifts and calling and made a new set of connections, we began attracting some college students, but not when we tried to address that challenge head on.

Eric Reis says there is no greater destroyer of creative potential than choosing to persevere when we should pivot.[19] Organizations that cannot pivot get badly stuck, no matter how eloquent their mission statements are, or how much they care, or how biblical their commitments are. Leaders who cannot pivot find that their transition into ministry has stalled as well. On the other hand, new pastors who can begin learning the importance of pivoting in their ministries will experience an overflow of that importance into their own lives and move through the transition into ministry with more momentum and command.

Risk and vulnerability will characterize a lot of your transition into ministry. Some days you will want to hide in the shadows

19. Reis, *Lean Start-Up*, 11.

and even disappear because you cannot find the emotional energy and spiritual stamina to risk conflict for the sake of something important or to show vulnerability in a setting where you already feel too overextended. The practice of agility keeps you growing and moving forward—intellectually, pastorally, and spiritually—and that is crucial during this transition. Agility will propel you to explore new leadership strategies, to appreciate the nimbleness that is available in lean situations, and to awaken risk and adventure as you situate yourself closer and closer to the action. The pivots you will make in all these areas will contribute positively and meaningfully to your transition into ministry.

How Agility Relates to the Other Practices

Though sometimes people use agility and nimbleness interchangeably, nimbleness is more than agility by itself. Agility can be reduced to reactionary, frenetic, random, urgent movement toward the latest idea. While nimbleness includes agility, it is fueled by curiosity and temerity, directed by clarity, and leads to proximity.

For example, an agile curiosity transforms casual exploration and detached musings into active discernment and purposeful adventure. A similar result occurs when clarity is paired with agility. Clarity contributes direction and focus to agility. Agility ensures proximity by moving us closer to the action, and ensures that once we are there our proximity translates into participation and not just observation. Agility moves those who otherwise might do nothing more than stew and fret at home—or church—into the arena where nerve can work on engaging issues, claiming opportunities, changing lives, and uplifting communities.

Without agility, on the other hand, nimbleness loses its energy and, therefore, its impact. Our thoughts may never find voice and our values may never manifest themselves in action. Without agility, curiosity may yield some provocative conversations and breed some really interesting study groups, but those ideas will fail to find expression in the church and community. If our clarity about a social or theological issue remains in our hearts and minds and never moves into practice, then our discernment and preparation have been largely wasted. Without agility, it won't matter how close we stay to issues because we will be immobilized. And apart from agility, our temerity turns into regret and sadness over what might have been.

7

Proximity

I have spent my life watching, not to see beyond the world, merely to see, great mystery, what is plainly before my eyes. I think the concept of transcendence is based on a misreading of creation. With all respect to heaven, the scene of the miracle is here, among us.[1]

—MARILYNNE ROBINSON

This is not work for hire
by this expenditure
you make yourself a place;
you make yourself a way
for love to reach the ground.[2]

—WENDELL BERRY

NOAH KNEW THAT HE would miss the strong, steady support of his seminary community once he graduated, but he was unprepared for the depth of isolation he would experience in his first

1. Robinson, *Death of Adam*, 243.
2. Berry, *This Day*, 120.

few years of ministry. Part of the isolation was geographical. The small Oklahoma town where he moved is a two-hour drive from frequent cultural events and major medical services. It was a fourteen-hour drive back to the town where he grew up, a town where most of his family and closest friends still lived. Another part of the isolation was holding in his heart and spirit the many difficult situations he encountered through his pastoral care, none of which he could speak about with anybody in the church and community. Still another part of the loneliness came with the leadership decisions that pastors face. Even though Noah made very few unilateral decisions, he recognized that he had a unique perspective on many of the situations by virtue of being the pastor. He also felt a certain seclusion when he wondered what repercussions and criticisms he might face from those who disagreed with him on key decisions.

Noah recognized that his loneliness was playing out in several directions. The isolation he felt as a person bled over into his pastoral demeanor and work, and the isolation he experienced as a pastor created distance from his own spouse and children. At the same time, the congregation grew more isolated every year, turning increasingly inward from the community around it. He joined an online clergy group, which put him in touch with people having similar experiences. Then he and his wife set aside three times each week just to talk with each other and stay connected. With toddlers in the house, this was no easy accomplishment. He spoke candidly about his feelings of isolation with his wife. She shared many of the same feelings. They renewed their pledge to make this journey together, to be open and honest with one another about the highs and lows of the journey, and to make sure that the family members' support of one another was visible to the congregation. Then they did one more thing. Seeking a way to become a part of the community, they began volunteering at the local elementary school, tutoring first and second graders in reading and writing. The isolation of being a pastor never completely goes away, but Noah and his family leaned into the issue and sought ways to become involved rather than withdraw further. Doing so changed how they saw their new community, how they saw each other, and how they saw themselves.

PROXIMITY AS A PRACTICE

Stephen Biko was a young South African protester and poet in the anti-apartheid struggle in South Africa. Before being assassinated in 1977 at the age of thirty, he wrote,

> In order to achieve real action you must yourself be a living part of Africa and of her thought; you must be an element of the popular energy which is entirely called forth for the freeing, the progress and the happiness of Africa. There is no place outside of that fight for the artist or for the intellectual who is not himself concerned with, or completely at one with, the people in the great battle of Africa and of suffering humanity.[3]

Biko believed that only those who live close enough to the life of a people can appreciate fully the dreams and fears of the people and of a given place. Those who are consistently present in the life of a people and the life of a community understand the realities, engender trust, and bring possibilities that have gone unnoticed. Forty years after his assassination, Steve Biko's love for South Africa continues to give life to his homeland.

Only when we become part of a community's energy or heartache will we bring to bear the needed gifts and perspectives. People are discerning. They know whether we are part of the fabric of a community or not. They can tell the extent to which our gifts and perspectives are informed and shaped by the opportunities and needs of a community. If our gifts and perspectives congealed long ago into a neat package that does not make room for the aspirations and concerns of one's current community, people will notice the separation.

For new pastors dealing with the effects of isolation, becoming part of the life of a place accomplishes one more thing: it keeps

3. Biko, *I Write What I Like*, 32.

you moving through the transition into ministry. The isolation cannot be taken lightly. Many capable and effective new pastors have not overcome the isolation of the early years of ministry. Some moved to another congregation or agency and essentially restarted the transition. Still others stepped away from ministry, sometimes for good, because the isolation on top of all the other factors at play during the transition became too great an emotional and spiritual burden to address at the time.

In other words, if you are feeling isolated at this point, you are in good company. It's part of the transition. Your new town or city does not include the familiar landmarks and memories of prior years. Your family may reside several states away. In some cases, your family may only reside several counties away, but during this transition, the distance is measured more by questions and emotions than by miles. Contact with friends wanes. You are learning a new culture and different community rhythms. You are finding strange differences in the way public services are organized and accessed. And of course, in the midst of many changes, you are doing the dance of finding your place (without losing yourself!) in a new web of relationships that comes with starting at a congregation or agency.

It's no wonder that new pastors feel isolated. We can only handle so many new things. At many points along the way, we have to pause and process what we are experiencing. Introverts will find this even more exhausting, but most everyone finds at some point that tending to our own well-being during a major transition consumes a lot of time and energy. In other words, part of moving through this transition well can lead to an experience of isolation as we emotionally step back to sort through all the new things that come with this change. Just managing ourselves can consume our days. It's important to name the various angles of isolation that are a normal part of your transition.

At the same time, some of you will deal with particular experiences that can ratchet up the feelings of isolation. For example, Carie was appointed to serve a congregation that had never had a female pastor, much less one who was single. The dimensions of her transition intertwined with those of the congregation. Jorge began a Spanish-speaking ministry in a community where only English was spoken in the schools and businesses. The members of his congregation already faced changes beyond what most Americans can appreciate as they tried to navigate the challenges of life in a new country. Jorge couldn't separate the emotions of his transition into ministry from serving a community for whom the changes have just begun. Justin, a gay man, was called to serve a church in a town where the county clerk had taken her objection to gay marriage all the way to the US Supreme Court. He had known isolation most of his life anyway. To see a core part of his identity being debated in the public square added unexpected layers to an already long list of concerns about beginning a new ministry. Scenarios like these greatly exacerbate the isolation that comes with the transition into ministry.

What matters is how we approach the experience of isolation during the transition into ministry. The temptation will be to withdraw into deeper separation, but that will only complicate and delay your transition. You should still set aside time for processing and reflection, as well as generous amounts of time under the theme of "being good to yourself." Doing so will help you be in touch with your emotions and the internal shifts that are a part of this transition. It also will cause you to prioritize carefully and prayerfully how you spend your time in ministry.

But in the end, you cannot sequester yourself from your own ministry. You will move through the isolation that is part of this transition by practicing proximity. Jesus didn't say, "Go set up a booth somewhere and if people stop by, do what you can for them." He didn't lead them into the temple; he sent them into the world. "Take the good news to the villages," Jesus said. We have always been the "sent," sent toward the action, sent toward possible partners, sent toward what claims us, sent toward the new world God has proposed. "As the Father has sent me," Jesus said, "so I send you."[4]

4. John 20:21.

A lot of congregations are sitting back, still waiting on people to come to them. They pour their energy into propping up cumbersome committee structures, fixing up old buildings, and tending to details that do not have even a remote connection to the realm of God, all the while losing sight of their vocation and focusing increasingly on their own survival. And their pastors wait around day after day in comfortable studies, waiting on the action to come to them, but it never does because they aren't at one with the community. If they were, the joys of the community would be their joys and the cries of the community would be their cries.

A few years ago, some people started talking about what it means to be missional—missional congregations, missional leaders, missional regions and conferences and denominations. This is how caught up in itself the church has become. When people started talking about being missional, much of the church was so inwardly focused that it sounded like a new idea!

You are being sent to give witness to the hope and healing God desires for all the world. To do that, you will need proximity to the opportunities as well as to the pain that exists not very far beyond the doorsteps of the church.

We are called to look always to the growing edge, as Howard Thurman said. Old worlds are dying everyday and new worlds are being born. Look to the growing edge.[5] More than that, go and stand at the growing edge, point it out to the rest of us, and call us to engage what is emerging so that we can help shape its character and its possibilities.

I will tell you in advance that life on the growing edge can be hard at times. For all their talk about wanting leaders who teach and model the faith, congregations usually reward managers who keep things running smoothly and unchanged, no matter the opportunities and challenges that lie all around us. If that's what you encounter, remember that a significant part of looking to the growing edge is about your transition into ministry. If an agency engages its mission with new clarity and energy or if a congregation renews its practices of worship, learning, and hospitality,

5. Thurman, *Growing Edge*, inside cover.

praise God! But in this discussion, I am encouraging you to look to the growing edge of the life of your community because it will lift the horizons on the growing edge of your transition into ministry. Your steady and (hopefully) adventurous engagement with what is going on around you will help you deal with what is going on within you. The isolation will not be eliminated, nor should it be, but it can be seen in its proper light as an aspect of ministry and as a reality of this transition, rather than an insurmountable challenge to your personhood and your work.

Think with me about how proximity plays out in Scripture. Isaiah 11, for example, says, "The cow and the bear shall graze, their young shall lie down together; and the lion shall eat straw like the ox. The nursing child shall play over the hole of the asp, and the weaned child shall put its hand on the adder's den. They will not hurt or destroy on all my holy mountain."[6] We can't get much closer to the action than putting our hand over the adder's den.

Or consider this passage from 1 Thessalonians: "But we were gentle among you, like a nurse tenderly caring for her own children. So deeply do we care for you that we are determined to share with you not only the gospel of God but also our own selves, because you have become very dear to us."[7] We do not become dear to each other or to a place from a distance, partly because until we live with the foibles and delights of a place we don't know it as truly as we do up close and over time. It's only when we are up close that we can give ourselves to each other and to a community.

A dinner with Jesus was interrupted once because a woman bathed Jesus' feet with her tears and then dried them with her hair. That's not an everyday occurrence, but the question Jesus asked when those around him were offended goes to the heart of the practice of proximity: "Do you see this woman?"[8] Are you close enough to the life of a place to actually see it as it is and not as you want or need for it to be? Are you skewing your view of a place by imposing something from your own life and perspective on it?

6. Isa 11:7–9a.
7. 1 Thess 2:7b–8.
8. Luke 7:44.

My favorite story involves ear wax. Some people brought a deaf man to Jesus. Jesus created a little privacy for the man and then stuck his fingers into the man's ears. Then he spat and touched his tongue. "Be opened," Jesus said, "and immediately [the man's] ears were opened, his tongue was released, and he spoke plainly."[9] You can't get much closer than putting your fingers in somebody else's ears. Maybe that is the gauge of proximity! If you have ear wax on your fingers, or the scent of protest on your breath, or the smell of marginalization on your clothes, or the echoes of the poor and left-out ringing in your ears, you have probably been practicing proximity. You don't get those things from a distance. And if you have been practicing proximity, it's likely that your isolation has diminished to a manageable level.

Now, because I know how easily some will interpret my words about proximity as dancing dangerously close to sacred boundaries and not caring well enough for oneself, let's talk about what proximity is not. Proximity doesn't mean smothering a place with your presence by being always present at everything. It certainly is not a path by which you get your needs, emotional or otherwise, met. Proximity to a community does not mean you lose yourself and your identity by becoming a part of its life. Nor is it a way to avoid the important role you play at your congregation or agency.

Rather, the practice of proximity fosters a life where you live. Isolation can turn us inwardly upon ourselves. It also can cause us to exaggerate how wonderful the place was where we lived previously. Gail Godwin writes in her novel *Evensong*,

> The human mind, as we know from personal experience, is a chronic time traveler, but we are repeatedly amazed by its ability to hitch up the body, the body that resides the only place it can—in present time—and pull it along like a wagon, with its entire load of sensory equipment, backward or forward into other time zones.[10]

9. Mark 7:34b–35.
10. Godwin, *Evensong*, 88.

The temptation during the transition into ministry is to let our minds have their way, to let them take us backward into some familiar time and place or forward into an idealized situation that likely doesn't exist. But moving well through the transition involves setting our bodies into the particulars of a community and hitching our minds to the specifics of that time and place.

Proximity helps you get planted into the same soil in which everyone else is growing around you and, thus, to put the isolation in a healthy perspective. The isolation is real, but it doesn't have to be personally debilitating and ministry ending. Earlier I mentioned Stafford's quote about finding out what the world is trying to be. During the transition into ministry, the work is even more personal as we try to find what we are trying to be. Practicing proximity contributes to that discovery.

KEY OPPORTUNITIES TO PRACTICE PROXIMITY

Proximity to your calling.

Remember what caused you to consider this vocational path in the beginning. It probably wasn't because you found the status quo so helpful and fulfilling. Rather, you likely wanted to help people experience God's love and hope. You probably wanted to know the joys of leading a faith community. You wanted to ease the suffering and to make it easier for weary and frustrated people to access the spiritual and material resources they most need. Too often, it seems, seminary becomes a disruption that makes connecting one's life prior to seminary with one's life after seminary nearly impossible. Fortunately, that is not always the case, and people do experience seminary as a deepening of one's faith and practice, but the seminary experience often does not safeguard the joy that people first felt when a call to ministry began to stir within them. Stay spiritually, emotionally, and physically close to what set you on this path and what renews you day by day to continue on this path. This means allowing who you are to fill the pastoral role, rather than emptying yourself of all that makes you beautiful and authentic and then being refilled with all the proper seriousness of the pastoral role.

Stay close to the joy, to the fun, to whatever enlivens you and makes you real. Stay close to those aspects of the faith that register with you and animate your energy. We are followers first—disciples, learners, explorers, protesters, pray-ers. We dare to lead week after week because we take seriously our followership. Adventurous ministry is born of adventurous followership. Vulnerability is required to hear a call to ministry. We are vulnerable when we are laughing and crying and opening our hearts to one another. We are vulnerable when we are uncomfortable and in uncharted territory, spiritually or geographically. We discern God's voice and claim on our lives more readily in that vulnerability, so even now, in a transition saturated with vulnerability, remain open to the Holy within and around you so that you can stay in close proximity to your calling.

Proximity to the people making this journey with you.

Since it is different for each person, let's begin by asking who is on this journey with you. Do you have a spouse or partner? Children? Are you caring for an aging parent while serving in your ministry? Who else is physically and emotionally close enough to be considered a fellow traveler? Now that you are reminded of who is making this journey with you, assess what you do to stay connected with those persons and how well it is working. It's a sign of trouble if you know more about the school activities of the youth in your church than what your own kids are doing. It's a sign of grave concern if conversations with people at church occur with greater ease, enjoyment, and intimacy than the conversations with your spouse do.

We can disconnect on so many levels. Usually the emotional and spiritual disconnect leads to a distance in physical intimacy, which in turn can lead to relationships ending. Just like it is easier to prevent ministry burnout than recover from it, it is easier to stay close to those on the journey with us than it is to restore those relationships once they are broken. David Augsburger says that being heard is so close to being loved that for the average person, they are almost indistinguishable.[11] Practicing proximity with those closest to you involves more than simply sitting in the same room day after day or even sleeping in the same bed night after night. It means remaining emotionally present and engaged, so much so that those in your own home feel heard. If Augsburger is right, they will simultaneously feel loved.

Cherish those making the journey with them. Express to them your appreciation for their support and your gratitude for the ways that make you feel heard and love. Show them the same support for their callings and interests that they offer for yours. Draw and preserve the boundaries necessary for a life together. In doing so, it's likely the clear commitments and the healthy enjoyment of your time away from church will positively impact the congregation or agency you are serving, but first do this for you and those closest to you. You do not want to exacerbate the isolation of this transition by creating even more distance between yourself and those you love.

Proximity to trusted ministry partners.

Recent seminary graduates can find themselves situated as solo pastors in struggling congregations, with limited collegial or institutional support. This can, and often does, result in a professional, relational, intellectual, and cultural isolation that can be detrimental to the formation of one's vocational identity. Just as staying close to those in your own home will enhance your transition, identifying and cultivating reliably trusting relationships will benefit you greatly as you steer through various changes and adjust emotionally and spiritually. Begin making relationships as if you think you will be in that community and at that congregation or agency forever. Develop them with care, integrity, and transparency. Remain current and available in those relationships, lest

11. Augsburger, *Caring Enough*, 148–71.

misunderstandings and disagreements deteriorate the trust you have worked so diligently to create.

Your relationship to those in your congregation or agency will be essential to effective leadership and a fulfilling ministry. Another circle of relationships will be with clergy colleagues in the area. Not many people experience local ministerial associations or large denominational gatherings as particularly life-giving, but it's important to stay in relationship with other clergy. What is likely is that there will be two or three out of a room of twenty pastors with whom you connect on a personal and professional level. Spend more time ensuring the quality of those relationships than trying to develop close ties with everyone present. The accompaniment of a small group of supportive, resonant colleagues can be an important catalyst in the transition into ministry.

Relationships at one's ministry site and with area-wide colleagues comprise nearly the whole network for some pastors. However, for you to realize the impact you desire for your ministry, you will want to look for creative partners and adventurous collaborators who live and work outside the usual clergy networks. These may be individuals involved in social enterprise or the arts, for example, or groups engaged with community organization and change. Too many pastors maintain a suspicious, prejudiced, and even an allergic distance from persons in business or government, even though those people often have the resources and willingness to support good causes. The pastoral task is to help those people understand how their values and commitments align with your ministry initiative so that their resources can be channeled for the well-being of the community, but that is difficult to do from a distance.

Proximity to what is emerging.

What opportunities are surfacing in your community? What interesting conversations are occurring? What crises are brewing? Pastors function in a representative way for the church. We study on behalf of others in order to preach and teach well, knowing that not everybody can set aside time for the same level of study. When we visit people in the hospital, we bring the care and support of the church into the room with us to envelop those who are struggling with illness. We function in a representative way also when we keep our eyes, ears, hearts, and minds open to see things that are emerging that no one else sees. You have been set apart for this very work!

The isolation during the transition into ministry wanes when we recognize that our voices and gifts are needed for what a community faces or for an opportunity that the community might seize. Most of these things will be slow in developing. Remember, for instance, the careful pace with which you discerned a call to ministry. Be prepared to tend to this new thing with the same care over a long period of time. Those who do not maintain a faithful proximity to what God is calling forth either will miss what is emerging or won't be trusted to nurse it along when it does begin to grow. Ray Bradbury says that if you give yourself to something, if you stay at it and with it, learn about it and learn from it, you might just learn a new word for work, and that word is love.[12] Proximity to what is emerging, whether it is opportunity or crisis, in the church or in the community, causes a love to grow that both brings your gifts and leadership into the service of what is emerging and eases the isolation that can so hamper a new ministry.

Proximity in relationship to the other practices of nimbleness.

Proximity makes the other practices relevant. It turns the curiosity of church study groups into lessons on discipleship. It fosters clarity by giving clarity a set of concrete circumstances where its convictions can take root and live. Proximity brings focus to agility, otherwise we will move in random directions that may or may not connect or impact the community. And proximity offers the opportunity to embody an untested, aspirational temerity in the

---

12. Bradbury, *Zen in the Art of Writing*, 4.

face of real challenges that matter to the congregation, agency, and community.

At the same time, proximity finds energy in the other four practices. Curiosity asks these questions of a place: "Who here are the unseen and unheard, and how are their lives being impacted? What possibilities are present that need to be uncovered and held up to the light?" Clarity presses proximity to move beyond vagueness in our desire to do good and in our assessment of a situation in order to get to the heart of an issue or opportunity. Once the heart of a matter is determined, agility moves us more fully into the matter, allowing us to be closer and closer for the sake of our understanding and contribution. And when we are clear and face-to-face with an opportunity for our congregation or agency to uplift a forgotten segment of the community, to protest a decision, or to care for a people in crisis, temerity causes us to act. Many people through the ages, including most of us, have been face-to-face with a challenge and have known what needed to happen, but a lack of temerity immobilized us. We turn toward the practice of temerity now.

8

Temerity

I did not shrink from declaring to you the whole purpose of God.[1]

—PAUL OF TARSUS

Bear in mind that one of the ways the Empire keeps us in bondage is by trivializing our dreams. The Empire badly wants us to dream small dreams [and] to be overly preoccupied with staying safe.[2]

—CARTER HEYWARD

Beware of ever finding a God totally congenial to you.[3]

—GAIL GODWIN

JENNIFER KNEW SHE WANTED to please and be accepted by others long before her transition into ministry began. As with many of us, she enjoyed the affirmation she received at home and in school and came to depend on it as one of her emotional supports. As

1. Acts 20:27; Paul is speaking to the elders at Ephesus.
2. Heyward, *Keep Your Courage*, 7.
3. Godwin, *Evensong*, 47.

an adult, Jennifer usually experienced a fairly low level of need of this affirmation, but during the transition into ministry she found herself hoping to be recognized and appreciated with greater frequency. On a few occasions, she found herself gauging how she was doing almost completely by the responses, affirmations, and criticisms of the people around her.

This seems fairly common among people in ministry, and it is particularly true during the transition into ministry while we are navigating the external and internal shifts described earlier. Even though we have spent years preparing for a time when we would lead a congregation or agency, everything can feel very new and even foreign. It's understandable that we are looking for clues about how we are doing. Church and community leaders receive wonderful expressions of support and praise from time to time, but the support and praise do not come in a steady stream. More often than not, the people in congregations and agencies love their pastors and directors, but they don't see propping up the emotional life of their pastors and directors as work that falls to them. This poses a common challenge during the transition into ministry. We don't expect others to consistently prop us up, but we do crave some signs and signals that our ministry is off to a good start and on the right track.

This dynamic gets really tricky when we get more response than we bargained for. When new pastors who are eager to please and do well in ministry encounter a small group—and it's almost always a small group—that manipulates pastors and dominates congregations and agencies, the potential for disaster is present. In her first congregation, Jennifer quickly found herself trying to walk a tightrope between pleasing a few key people and acting in the best interest of the congregation as a whole. She made occasional progress on congregationally established goals, but many times in the early days of her ministry felt like she and the congregation were being held hostage by two families. Over time, though, that changed as Jennifer exhibited temerity with her own learning and in her relationships with those who supported and challenged her alike.

TEMERITY AS A PRACTICE[4]

Scripture, of course, implores us in many other places to be courageous.[5] Consider the encouragement and instructions from the pastoral epistles of 1 and 2 Timothy and Titus. Those letters reflect both a care for the church and an expectation for those who would lead the church. It's true that parts of those letters deal with offices, roles, and organizational matters, but significant portions of those three letters focus on concerns like false teaching and diversionary discussions that take attention away from the gospel. The letters qualify church leaders in two ways. The first qualification, like that of a bishop, calls for a person who, among other things, is above reproach, temperate, sensible, and gentle. It focuses on managing and caring for people, especially their own families and the church.

The second set of qualifications does not appear so much in a list, but rather as themes that run through much of the pastoral letters. This is particularly true when the writer is appealing to young leaders in the church. At the heart of these themes is courage. In 2 Timothy, courage comes not from our own doing or genetics, but through our relationship with God. Second Timothy 1:7 makes it clear that our experience of God translates into a specific path related to courage and further implies that a less courageous path is not of God. For example, the Revised Standard Version of that verse reads, "for God did not give us a spirit of timidity but a spirit of power and love and self-control." The New International Version offers a similar phrase: "For the Spirit God gave us does not make us timid."

Later versions from those same translation families both make stronger statements. For example, the New International Reader's Version says this: "God gave us his Spirit. And the Spirit doesn't make us weak and fearful." The New Revised Standard Version

---

4. I've chosen to use the word "temerity" here. More common words with same meaning include courage, nerve, and audacity.

5. Deuteronomy 31:6-8, 1 Chronicles 28:20, John 14:27, and Ephesians 6:10 are examples that either name courage explicitly or otherwise suggest its centrality to the life of faith.

goes one step further: "for God did not give us a spirit of coward-ice, but rather a spirit of power and of love and of self-discipline."

There's not a good or right time to attempt to shut down the spirit of God within you. We wouldn't do that intentionally any-way, not after you experienced God's call to ministry and trusted God's sustaining presence during seminary, but new pastors often feel disconnected from their own spiritual lives at a time when they most need grounding, focus, and strength. In the experience of some new pastors, the transition into ministry issues we have named seem to override God's assurance and guidance. It should be the other way around. God's assurance and guidance should be what makes an adventurous, timely, and impactful transition into ministry possible and fulfilling. If you are feeling timid, fearful, or cowardly, a good starting place is to acknowledge those feelings as part of the human experience and part of the transition into ministry, but don't stop there. Continue to nurture and cultivate your spiritual life and your emotional well-being in ways that open your life to the fruit of the Spirit.

God is constantly present to us. That is true during every change. God gives life and hope, and in the process, possibilities emerge that help complete transitions for the sake of renewed in-dividuals and restored communities. I encourage you to consider a transition into ministry that is characterized not by timidity, fear or cowardice, but by audacity, courage and nerve.

Consider these examples of temerity from Scripture that can inform and encourage you in your transition into ministry. Let's begin with Jeremiah.

It was six hundred years before Jesus was born and Jerusalem, as it so often has been, was under siege.[6] The powerful Babylonians were destroying the holy city. In the midst of a hopeless military and political situation, Jeremiah did the strangest thing. He bought a piece of land.

Is that not the strangest, most ill-advised move you have ever heard of? Isn't that something like buying a townhouse in a war zone where no end to the fighting is in sight? Or seeing a hurricane

6. See Jeremiah 32.

form in the ocean and rushing out to purchase a beach house that sits in the direct path of the storm? Or going into a neighborhood where violence has left the streets blood-stained and acquiring a whole neighborhood of houses?

Everything, including the temple, was being destroyed. For those thinking in terms of return on investment, no reason could be found to think Jeremiah would ever be able to turn a profit on this piece of land. And for those thinking beyond just the dollars and cents of a real estate transaction, the possibility that his people would ever have a life in Jerusalem again seemed slim at best.

But that's the point. Jeremiah wasn't buying low. He wasn't looking to turn a profit. No, Jeremiah was making a courageous statement about the future, just as your temerity makes a courageous statement about your future in ministry. In the midst of disaster and destruction, Jeremiah bought a piece of land. It was a way of saying, "No calamity extinguishes the hope that comes from God. We'll be back. God will restore Israel's fortunes. We will worship in this holy city again. Houses and fields and vineyards shall again be bought in this land." Earlier in Jeremiah, we hear the lament that courage shall fail the king and the officials, but it did not fail Jeremiah.[7]

Temerity or courage is a dimension of nimbleness because so much of ministry depends on church and community leaders who can simultaneously attend to the present moment and, at the same time, take a longer view of the situation. This is especially the case during the transition into ministry, when so many immediate needs, both your own and those of people you serve, clamor for your time and attention. The temptation will often be to react only to what is right before you and to manage that issue. Sometimes our management of a particular day's issue isn't much more than closing down a conversation, or quickly appeasing someone with a complaint, or kicking the can of some decision down the road to another meeting.

Temerity causes us to stand back and take an honest look at the possibilities and circumstances before us. Our constructive engagement with them not only benefits the congregation or agency,

7. Jer 4:9–10; 19–28.

but it also contributes significantly to our transition into ministry and deters our inclination to please others at all costs.

In the Acts of the Apostles, Paul makes a bold statement to the elders at Ephesus. Twice he says, "I did not shrink." Paul says, "I did not shrink from doing anything helpful, proclaiming the message to you and teaching you publicly and from house to house."[8] And later in the same chapter: "for I did not shrink from declaring to you the whole purpose of God."[9]

Now, before we set the bar too high, let's confess that on some days and on some opportunities or issues, we likely will shrink. That is, very few of us measure up fully to a standard of always rising to the occasion. Forgetting that will make your transition even harder.

At the same time, Paul's words encourage us during this critical stage of life and ministry. With so much new in your life and so much uncertain in your ministry, shrinking comes easily. That's true with any change. There will be days when we most want to step away from the spotlight and fade into the woodwork. Because just dealing with our emotions during a transition can be a full-time job, it's understandable that engaging in the work and relationships of ministry will be more than we can do on some days. Pay attention to those and get some time away to reflect and rest so that you can re-engage later.

Later in Acts, Paul is described to the governor as a pestilent fellow, an agitator, and a ringleader.[10] Similar things were said of Jesus, who seemed fairly inattentive to maintaining a good reputation. Perhaps similar things will be said of you as you practice temerity during your transition. The goal, remember, is not to alienate people or to bring criticism on yourself, though that will surely happen at some point, but to keep your focus on your transition into ministry. The practice of temerity, of continuing to engage as your authentic self in the midst of various risks and

8. Acts 20:20.

9. Acts 20:27.

10. Acts 24:5.

vulnerabilities, will help you keep moving toward the completed transition that you seek and need.

In addition to these stories from Scripture, we find theological temerity expressed in the liturgy of the church. Consider this collect from the Book of Common Prayer:

> Keep, O LORD, your household the Church in your steadfast faith and love, that through your grace we may proclaim your truth with boldness, and minister your justice with compassion; for the sake of our Savior Jesus Christ, who lives and reigns with you and the Holy Spirit, one God, now and for ever. Amen.[11]

And again in the invitation to the LORD's Prayer, "And now, as our Savior Christ has taught us, we are bold to say, Our Father."[12]

Our worship life offers avenues by which our nerve can be nurtured. The collect asks for grace to proclaim God's truth with boldness, for which you will have many opportunities. Each one will move you more fully into and through your transition. The introduction to the LORD's Prayer acknowledges that even bowing before God in prayer can be a bold act. As Brother James Koester writes, "When you are . . . alone in prayer . . . find the threshold and step over it, find the border and cross it, and I assure you, you will find . . . God's divine presence even there, where you have been told that God could not possibly be."[13] This rhythm of proclaiming and acting boldly, on one hand, and praying boldly on the other, fosters courage during your transition by keeping you grounded and connected to the God who called you by name and who continues daily to give guidance and strength.

11. *Book of Common Prayer*, 230.

12. *Book of Common Prayer*, 336.

13. Koester, "Finding God in the Marsh," para. 18.

KEY OPPORTUNITIES FOR PRACTICING TEMERITY

Temerity toward oneself.

During the transition into ministry, we can vacillate between two extremes. On the one hand, we can spend endless hours in introspection, often arriving at far harsher conclusions about ourselves and our ministry than what is deserved. On the other, we can be carried along on other people's opinions and worldviews, rarely thinking for ourselves and often granting those opinions and worldviews far more weight than they deserve. A more helpful, life-giving path involves honest self-confrontation, and that takes courage. It is much easier to keep busy. We may even find ourselves creating distractions and diversions in order to avoid thinking about how we are doing as we consider the endings, neutral zones, and beginnings of this particular transition.

Find time every day to be vulnerable with yourself and to assess how you are doing. Allow these times to rekindle your spirit and your call to ministry. Look for the threshold between timidity and temerity and imagine ways that you can cross that threshold genuinely and hopefully. This will seem odd and awkward the first few times you do it, but with every fresh look at yourself, what you value, and what you are giving life to comes increased nerve to consider afresh the opportunities for ministry that exist before you. Brene Brown says that the most courageous act in the world is that of being vulnerable,[14] but from that act comes a reconnection with yourself and a reawakening to what matters most to your ministry. Practicing temerity, even with yourself, fosters temerity.

Temerity toward risk.

We know that risk is a part of life. It's inherent in every relationship and situation, to varying degrees. Risk also resides at the heart of the gospel. The servants Jesus celebrated in his parable

14. Brown, *Daring Greatly*, 292.

of the talents were those who risked what they had been given. The servant to whom the master spoke a harsh judgement was the one who hid his talent in the ground, even though he was able to return it in full later on.[15]

Do we dare reach out and risk rejection? Do we intentionally make the congregation or community uncomfortable about a need or issue in order to attempt something beautiful and life-giving? Do we continue down this transition into ministry road and risk things not working out later on. We can spend a lot of time calibrating risks and calculating losses.

Sometimes imagining where the risks play out remains a vague enterprise. Naomi, a new pastor who shares her story in a report on transition into ministry programs, describes the space that is needed "to risk being a minister in all its complexity, and saying, often with delight and some surprise, 'Well I can do this!'"[16] This revelation usually does not come to us in a single flash, but over time, as we practice temerity by practicing risk. This risk-taking occurs through our leadership of worship, our faithful preaching and teaching, our care of individuals and the congregation or agency we serve, and our engagement with the broader community as representatives of the gospel. In each case, we either choose words and actions that convey that the realm of God has come near, or we trivialize our faith with words and actions that allow our comfortable lives to continue without challenge and disruption.

It's frightening to risk much in a badly divided culture, especially if others don't seem to be risking very much. You don't have to overturn an evil empire in your first year of ministry. Rather, let our story, the Christian story, steadily do its work through your ministry. Each time you do that, you will be growing in temerity by practicing temerity.

---

15. Matt 25:14–30.

16. Scharen and Campbell-Reed, "Learning Pastoral Imagination," 26.

Temerity toward conflict.

Conflict provides an excellent example of the learning that can occur when new pastors truly engage opportunities and challenges during the transition into ministry. Conflict presents its own web of complex issues. In stagnant or complacent situations, conflict can be used to renew priorities. In other cases, conflict becomes an intentional wedge that drives people apart and undermines the mission of a congregation or agency. Few enjoy conflict. It's hard not to take things personally, so most people avoid conflict to one degree or another. Some still think of conflict as unchristian and do not believe that even the best facilitation of conflict can lead to anything good, but as Bishop Robert DeWitt said of his leadership regarding racial integration and the ordination of women to the Episcopal priesthood, "I had to decide where to stand, and neutrality was not, it seemed to me, an option."[17]

We all have certain styles of managing conflict.[18] Often, these approaches are learned early on as we watch how conflict plays out in our family of origin. One way to view the climate in which you are making your transition from seminary is to note the pervasive cultural polarization and decide that nothing good could come from engaging those conversations. In fact, you may be convinced that this engagement will cause you to be unemployed. You may be right, but another approach is at least worth considering. In the midst of this great divide, a lot of people crave honest discussion about important issues, and they seek guidance in how best to form positions on those issues from a faith perspective. In other words, you will stand in the midst of the division and suspicion and do what pastors do—help people interpret their lives in light of God's presence and purposes for them and for the whole world. The more often you practice temerity toward conflict during your transition into ministry, the more comfortable you will become with standing in the midst of emotionally charged conversations as one charged with the responsibility both to interpret and model the Christian life.

17. Heyward, *Keep Your Courage*, 172.

18. For a helpful description of common conflict management styles and an analysis of your own style, see Leas, *Discover Your Conflict Management Style.*

Temerity toward success.

Pastors, congregations, and not-for-profit agencies especially struggle with success. Notice what I said. I didn't say they struggle with becoming successful, though that is often the case. They struggle with the idea of success. Is it something we should seek because it could be one way to understand the impact of our ministry? Or is it something that we should shun because all notions of success involve greed, superficiality, exploitation, and misplaced priorities? And then, of course, what could be worse than Christian success? We are suspicious of success. After all, how do we square any idea of success with walking humbly with our God and leading a life of humility and gentleness?[19]

But surely we want our ministry to have impact, right? Even when the last thing on our minds is the attention or rewards that may come to us, we want our efforts to bless others. We also want the congregations and agencies that we serve to participate in God's transforming of the world.

Part of the challenge is that we need a new definition of success. Another part of the challenge, whether we call it success or choose an entirely different word for it, is that many pastors tend to be afraid of success. Marianne Williamson writes,

> Our deepest fear is not that we are inadequate. Our deepest fear is that we are powerful beyond measure. It is our light, not our darkness, that most frightens us. Your playing small does not serve the world. There is nothing enlightened about shrinking so that other people won't feel insecure around you. We are all meant to shine as children do. It's not just in some of us; it is in everyone. And as we let our own lights shine, we unconsciously give other people permission to do the same. As we are liberated from our own fear, our presence automatically liberates others.[20]

Instead of using the term success, let's call it flourishing in ministry, or having the time of our lives doing God's work, or

19. Mic 6:8; Eph 4:2.
20. Williamson, *Return to Love*, 190.

letting our light shine without fear or hesitation. Our ministry is offered for the glory of God and for the sake of the world. It's a wonderful thing to be part of. Playing small with our own light, though, causes us to get stuck during the transition into ministry and not fully realize its joy. You'll experience some wonderful moments as a new pastor. Resist the temptation of asking whether you deserve these and resist the fear of being found out. Celebrate the moments and enjoy them. And for the sake of the seasons to come, don't hold back. In your preaching and leading of worship, in your caring and leading, trust your light and let it shine.

Temerity in relationship to the other practices of nimbleness.

Temerity energizes the other four practices. Courageous questions focus our curiosity not on the next thing that will please a church member, but on what matters most. On determining what that is, courage breeds clarity so that the energy we give to an opportunity or issue will be so compelling that even the most intransigent church system will have difficulty derailing it. Nerve creates a restlessness in us that propels us into agile action and sustains us as we lead, confront, and comfort. And finally, temerity will not allow us to remain at a distance from that which is promising or challenging, but rather moves us into close proximity so that we can engage it up close.

In the same way, the other four practices contribute to temerity. Curiosity has led many young people to learn about the courage of protesters and marchers from Selma, Alabama to Cape Town, South Africa. Clarity identifies what we will give our lives to and helps us see the specific ways to channel our nerve in the church and community. Agility knows that injustice always will be with us, and so it prepares us to pivot toward the next opportunity to make God's love visible in the world. Proximity cultivates temerity by bringing us close enough to those who are hurting and left out to understand their plight, see their tears and hear their cries.

9

Restlessness and Resilience

Therefore, since it is by God's mercy that we are engaged in this ministry, we do not lose heart.[1]

Bring me on my way
and do not cease
to pull, push and urge me on.[2]

Life is not a journey to the grave with the intention of arriving safely in a pretty, well-preserved body, but rather to skid in broadside, thoroughly used up, totally worn out, and loudly proclaiming, "Wow! What a ride!"[3]

MOST NEW PASTORS STRUGGLE, even do battle, between restlessness on the one hand and resilience on the other. Early days in ministry are filled with nearly overwhelming questions, one of which

1. 2 Cor 4:1.
2. Bach, "St. John Passion."
3. Heyward, *Keep Your Courage*, 232.

is whether you will continue as a pastor. I hope this one doesn't persistently snag you, but it occupies a lot of emotional space for many. That's understandable. The uncertainty about a new place and a new ministry site, coupled with serious questions about your ability and your desire to do this work, leads numerous new pastors to assume within their first year that they must have misheard or misunderstood their call. Any relocation involves many changes, and the stress of those logistics begins to add up. Each individual change becomes a reminder of the emotional strain of even a few transitions. Instead of leading a church or agency, you find yourself trying to contain and manage your own emotions. When even a few of the common challenges surface, such as stymied creativity, profound isolation, or the excessive desire to please people, it is only natural to at least entertain the idea of disconnecting from all things new and returning as quickly as possible to more familiar people and to safer surroundings. Sometimes the restlessness subsides to a manageable level. In other cases, people leave their church or agency, sometimes abruptly, and move to another ministry site or leave ministry altogether.

I do not personally know of anyone who reports that the restlessness has ever completely gone away. I recognize that is not the news you want to hear at this point in your pastoral journey, but it may be the news you need to receive. There's something about grappling with the presence of a disruptive God that fosters some restlessness. Were Jesus to be the destination instead of the way, or a room instead of a door, a prescription instead of the truth, we might feel more settled.[4] If ministry itself felt a little more defined and a lot less messy, or if it offered more finished products and less unfinished business, we might arrive at a satisfying pace much more easily. Or if our faith and discipleship could be parsed out and compartmentalized so that it did not require all our hearts and all our minds and all our souls,[5] then perhaps this restlessness would be compartmentalized as well, and the other parts of our lives wouldn't be affected and complicated by God's claim on our

4. John 10:9; 14:6.
5. Luke 10:27.

lives. In other words, not only is restlessness here to stay to some degree, it is a sign that you are invested and that all this matters to you.

The result of your investment is that restlessness is accompanied by resilience. Part of resilience comes from our own personal stamina and drive. The more enduring quality of resilience is derived from an ongoing relationship to the Holy that nurtures life and trust within us. Resilience is not lowering our head and pushing through until we have nothing left to give, but rather the calm confidence that comes from believing we did, in fact, hear the call of God and the church correctly and are now pursuing the vocational path we believe to be our own.

Now, that's not to say that you won't have days and weeks when enthusiasm has waned and the best you can do is put one foot in front of the other and keep moving. Ministry can be a cruel lover and the church can be a frustrating partner. As an alumna of our school once told me, "I learned to preach during seminary and to preach well. What I was not prepared for was having to preach with a broken heart." But that pastor demonstrates exceptional pastoral imagination and effectiveness because her resilience is grounded in the knowledge that she is serving the promises of God in her ministry. She displays a vocational trust—a trust in her call, if you will—that gives rise to a resilient spirit. More than that, she knows that she would not have chosen this path on her own, but was called to it and nurtured in it by a great cloud of witnesses and fellow travelers.

You will live with restlessness and resilience often during your transition into ministry. Neither of these will go away, but hear the good news in that statement. While the restlessness now may seem all consuming, it will even out over time. When it does, the restlessness that remains will be an experience of the disruptive faith you have in a God who is obsessed with making all things new, just, and peaceful. At some point, the restlessness brought on by personal changes and early professional challenges will become the fuel for your pastoral and prophetic voice that, in turn, points toward the new creation and calls others to participate in its coming. Before you know it, you will be using restlessness to gauge whether you are stirring up enough trouble for the gospel's sake and you'll become suspicious of your own ministry when it no longer unsettles you or anybody else.

> The hymn says,
> Spirit, spirit of restlessness
> Stir me from placidness,
> Wind, wind on the sea.[6]

Resilience offers the same kind of standard. With the call to ministry comes God's provision to endure difficult days of discouragement and resentment, but we shouldn't cast this only in the negative. Resilience will be key as you dream about opportunities and implement ministries that will enliven your congregation and agency and bless the community around you. That makes these five practices all the more valuable because they keep you close to your call to ministry during a transition full of oversized expectations, tempting distractions, and new beginnings of various kinds. Just as congregations and agencies gripped by anxiety seem unable to access their own faith story, so it is with individuals, including new and seasoned pastors. We sometimes deal in holy things, but do not feel their mystery or know their power. Even though transitions cause us to call into question nearly everything, trusting your call and allowing the cumulative effect of these practices to engender confidence in the midst of changes will help you to persevere and enjoy God's life-giving resilience in your life.

RESTLESSNESS IS REAL

The world became aware of Mother Teresa's restlessness after her death. At times, her restlessness apparently devolved into depression and a crisis of faith. Her presence and commitment to the poor of Calcutta demanded an amazing resilience, but we shouldn't move too quickly to that focus, lest we discount her long stretches of restlessness. It's important and valuable to normalize

6. Manley, "Spirit."

restlessness as something we all experience. You may be a little embarrassed that you are just now starting out in ministry and are already feeling restless, but think again about the many changes you have encountered and pushed through. How could you not feel some restlessness? I would wonder how empathic you could be to others if you weren't feeling some disquiet.

Much of the unsettledness can be traced to the depth and pace of emotions associated with the three stages of transition that we discussed in chapter one. You have experienced several endings and likely still have a few left to bring to conclusion. Endings leave us feeling separated and cut off. A future we once assumed belonged to us now seems unlikely. At the same time, you are engaged in so many beginnings, not the least of which is your work as pastor. You likely have moved to a new community, perhaps enrolled children in a new school, and are getting acquainted with everything from a new dentist to a new plumber. Newness greets you at every turn, even as you feel the emotional impact of numerous endings.

Neutral zones, that in-between time needed for processing, introspection, and appraising, have gotten compressed because you have had so many endings and beginnings occur in such close proximity to each other. That compression has left you little time to process the endings. As a result, even though you are giving your best effort to these many beginnings, the processing wheels continue to turn, and as they do, they bring up unresolved questions and lingering doubts.

Remember that, during times of change, unresolved questions and lingering doubts do not pose a mortal threat to one's vocational path or pastoral career. Rather, they are signs that the endings and beginnings came close together and your system is trying to catch up on the processing. Give the same gift of patience to yourself that you are giving to others.

E. L. Doctorow compared writing a novel to driving at night in the fog. We can only see as far as the headlights will allow us to see.[7] According to Doctorow, though, that's far enough, but in

7. Frequently mentioned by E. L. Doctorow. See, as examples, *Writers at*

the transition into ministry—not to mention the rest of life—it's natural to want more of a line of sight on things. This is new; you understandably want to know how it all turns out, and you would like to know that now!

Your restlessness can lead you to think early on about leaving your current ministry and going to a new one, but first do everything you can, including finding days when you do nothing at all, to put those thoughts in perspective. I caution you against a hasty decision for two reasons. First, another move will bring more endings and beginnings and likely further crowd out time and emotional space for reflection. Second, as we've discussed already, certain things undermine the learning that can and needs to occur during this transition. Moving too quickly to a second ministry position is one of those.

There's not a predetermined number of years to remain in your first ministry position, but fewer than four years or so can limit the opportunities needed to nurture the first stages of pastoral identity and imagination. As a result, understanding and managing your restlessness is critical. That really is a key part of this particular season's work for you.

And then, even in your restlessness, trust the cumulative work done well on a daily and weekly basis. You do not have to create sensational programs with spectacular results. Be a pastor. Teach, preach, serve, administer the Sacraments, and let the faith story do its work on you and on the people of your congregation or agency. As 2 Timothy 4 says, "Be persistent whether the time is favorable or unfavorable . . . with the utmost patience."[8]

RESILIENCE IS A PRACTICE

When Moses died, the community eulogized him with the highest praise. "His sight was unimpaired and his vigor had not abated . . . He was unequaled for all the signs and wonders that the

---

Work: *The Paris Review Interviews*, numbers 8, 22, and 94.

8. 2 Tim 4:2.

LORD sent him to perform in the land of Egypt, against Pharaoh and all his servants and his entire land, and for all the mighty deeds and all the terrifying displays of power that Moses performed in the sight of all Israel."[9]

That's an inspiring account of Moses' life, but Moses didn't start out displaying mighty deeds and performing signs and wonders. Moses didn't begin with unabated vigor. Early on, there was little indication that Moses would even say yes to God's call, much less go head-to-head with Pharaoh's oppressive regime to lead the people out of slavery. Moses encountered all sorts of restlessness and doubt, beginning with his conversation with God at the burning bush and continuing through much of his vocation as a liberator. In the end, though, we are told that he finished well. Moses pressed through his questions about whether he was the right person for this work and through the ongoing challenges of leading a stiff-necked and divided people. We call that resilience, and it's a key feature not just of the transition into ministry, but of thriving in ministry over many seasons.

People call forth and demonstrate resilience in different ways. Some personality types seem to quickly summon the fortitude to rise to the next challenge. It's like they have a storehouse of determination and are just waiting to learn where to apply it next. Others of us eventually gather ourselves and resume the journey, but we may stew and brood over the task for a long time before we ever give serious effort to getting started. Most people fall somewhere in between those two extremes. Personality can play a significant role, but our social location and what we have experienced in our lives contributes as well. No one gets to the transition-into-ministry stage without having already exhibited resilience. Seminary alone represents a huge test of resilience, as do other parts of our lives. Remember how you summoned strength, persistence, calm, and courage in other seasons and circumstances and, in whatever way is natural and constructive for you, call forth that resilience in this season. Perhaps you immediately announce to the world that you are taking on this challenge without hesitation. Others will

9. Deut 34:7b, 11, 12.

quietly assess the situation, reflect on its possibilities, and then engage slowly. Still others will consult with friends, prayer partners, and mentors. And still others may say very little, but continue moving forward with a steady but unassuming confidence.

While you draw on your personal resilience, remember too that not everything about this venture's success depends on you. We forget that sometimes. Just as stuck and dysfunctional congregations and agencies can't seem to access their own faith story, so it is with individuals, including new pastors. We handle holy things and present and re-present the sacred to those around us, but do not always internalize what we say. You are resilient, and God is with you.

> Do not fear, for I have redeemed you; I have called you by name, you are mine. When you pass through the waters, I will be with you; and through the rivers, they shall not overwhelm you; when you walk through fire you shall not be burned, and the flame shall not consume you. For I am the LORD your God.[10]

Call on your own personal experience of resilience and invoke the promises of God's presence and strength during this transition. At the same time, resilience is also a practice, and so here I offer ways to practice resilience during this transition into ministry and beyond.

First, nurture your resilience by staying close to your path. Celebrate the paths of others, but do not spend much time comparing your ministry to theirs. Chances are that your colleagues in ministry are every bit as restless as you are. There's neither time or reason to be envious. Your physical, emotional, and spiritual energy needs to be invested in managing your restlessness, reminding yourself of what led you to this calling in the first place, and focusing on the ministry before you. Your authenticity as a person and a pastor will emerge more fully as a result.

Second, your resilience will gain momentum as you stay close to what energizes you and keep to a minimum, while still

10. Isa 43:1b–3a.

performing your pastoral responsibilities, those people, tasks, and situations that drain you. In other words, don't make this harder on yourself than it already is! What energizes and what drains varies from person to person. It may even vary for you from one season of life or ministry to another. For example, it's not uncommon for the first few years in ministry to coincide with the first few years of parenting. Both of those endeavors bring profound joy and fulfillment, but they also both carry very taxing demands.

And be reminded of Jesus' invitation and promise:

> Are you tired? Worn out? Burned out on religion? Come to me. Get away with me and you'll recover your life. I'll show you how to take a real rest. Walk with me and work with me—watch how I do it. Learn the unforced rhythms of grace. I won't lay anything heavy or ill-fitting on you. Keep company with me and you'll learn to live freely and lightly.[11]

Third, nurture your resilience by staying close to people who have lived through a few more seasons than you have. Prominently placed on a bookshelf in my study is a picture of Anna Kingcade at her hundredth birthday party, which occurred when I was about forty. Anna was a member of the congregation I was serving at the time. I was glad and honored to be her pastor and to journey with her through days of both delight and challenge. My role was to be Anna's pastor, but on nearly every visit with her I came away with a gift that I cherished for my own days of delight and challenge—the gift of the long view.

On many days, Anna's panoramic view provided a much needed antidote to my myopic one. Anna's perspective, which dated to her birth in 1906, gave me a frame into which that week's trials—or even that year's trials!—could find its rightly proportioned dimensions. While I was likely painting the next five years as exceedingly and maybe even excruciatingly pivotal, Anna had lived through twenty sets of the five-year time frames. Her gift of perspective created breathing space, time to laugh at how seriously

11. Matt 11:28–30 (MSG).

I was taking myself, and an invitation to stop worrying about two years from now and instead work at being present in that moment and in that place.

Be good to yourself by connecting with people who can share this gift with you. As a new pastor, seek out a pastor who is in year twenty or thirty of her ministry. And then broaden your view with people from other perspectives, experiences, and professions. Anna wasn't a pastor—she was the executive assistant at a law firm for sixty years. I'm not sure how well she could have articulated what it's like to be in ministry, but sweeping stories and poignant reflections flowed from her like fresh water from a trusted spring. With sufficient self-awareness and appropriate emotional and physical boundaries, of course, put yourself in the company of people like Anna. Just being alongside them and listening to their stories allows for a longer view, which cultivates a special kind of resilience.

Fourth, learn to ask for help. Those in the so-called "helping professions" are notoriously reluctant to ask for help themselves. Take congregational pastors, for instance. They ask people for about anything at anytime. "Will you take the lead on this project?" "Will you increase your financial giving to the church?" "Will you join me at a public hearing about an abandoned neighborhood in our community?" "Will you go with me to the school board meeting where racial inequality is on the agenda?" But they have a hard time asking for help for themselves.

It's a gift to be strong and scrappy, but human finitude and frailty comes to us all at some point. The greater gift is to be human with each other, to be as open to receiving help as we are eager to give it, and to allow a community's care and companionship to laugh away the most debilitating mistake of all—that of not asking for help.[12] This is difficult when new pastors are already over-functioning, but we cannot make this journey by ourselves. Nor does anyone expect us to do so. I have heard dozens of our graduates report almost exactly the same story. The new pastor says, "I am struggling to balance my personal and family life with

12. See my article "Mistake" in the Buechner Narrative Writing Project.

the demands of being pastor," and the leaders respond, "How can we help?" Unfortunately, I also have heard many report that they never asked for help and left that congregation or agency as a result and, in some cases, left ministry altogether.

All new pastors need and deserve support and advocacy from their judicatory leaders and from a strong, trusted pastoral relations group within their congregation or agency, but you may need to make it clear exactly what support you are seeking. Many find that the most valuable support and advocacy come from trusted peers, either one-on-one or through a clergy peer group. Collegiality builds resilience and, interestingly, resilience builds collegiality. Even then, we will miss it if we do not avail ourselves of it when it is offered and ask for it when it isn't offered.

Fifth, make room for recovery experiences. Even the most hopeful and resilient among us will find ourselves at crossroads from time to time, weighing whether we are experiencing enough positives to keep the negatives from getting us down. For this, I call your attention to Matt Bloom's research on well-being at work.[13] Bloom contends that we know what well-being does not look like. We are well acquainted with the negatives, such as anxiety and depression, but we know little about the positives. For instance, to examine an oft-used phrase in this book, what does "flourishing in ministry" look like? The answer usually isn't to work harder and recklessly extend ourselves to the point of no return, but to think intentionally and creatively about two sources of well-being—hedonic and eudaimonic. Hedonic well-being is about sheer fun, pleasure and enjoyment. Eudaimonic well-being is derived from understanding one's work as meaningful and contributive.[14]

At the heart of Bloom's study are recovery experiences. When we experience a three-to-one ratio of positive experiences to negative ones, we maintain our moods and feelings. If we are able to reach a four- or even five-to-one ratio of positive to negative, our happiness increases. However, when we drop below the three-to-one ratio and only experience two-to-one or even one-to-one

13. See Bloom, "About," http://wellbeing.nd.edu/about/.

14. See Bloom, "Flourishing in Ministry," 7–8.

positive to negative experiences, our happiness decreases. And if you have one really bad experience, you likely need three really good ones to counter the bad one.[15]

Negative experiences include intractable conflict in the congregation or agency, chronically stressful situations such as personnel or other matters, negative relationships with other pastors and judicatory leaders, radical shift in the demands and expectations people have of our work, and experiences we construe as threats to our pastoral identity and authority. The more negative experiences we encounter over time, the more recovery experiences we need. Bloom describes recovery experiences as detachments and relaxation during each day, a restorative niche of mystery and enjoyment, spiritual practices (especially meditation and contemplation), positive challenges in ministry that evoke excitement, and quality relationships with other pastors and judicatory leaders.[16]

A BLESSING FOR THE TRANSITION

Yes, moving from the title of a poem to its first few lines is like stepping into a canoe. And yes, moving from seminary to your first ministry after seminary is like that, too. Jennifer and Noah stepped into that canoe. The canoe rocked for a while, but they eventually pushed away from the dock. They experienced smooth sailing for a while, then hit some rapids, steered clear of rocks and brush, and finally emerged in the clear for another stretch of relatively smooth sailing. Thousands of seminary graduates embark on this journey every year in the United States. All of them encounter challenges and, though not perfectly or elegantly, push through and eventually live into their new horizon.

One of John O'Donohue's blessings invites us to cross the thresholds of our lives worthily.[17] I have written this book to help you cross the threshold of the transition into ministry worthily.

15. Bloom, "Flourishing in Ministry," 19–20.
16. Bloom, "Flourishing in Ministry."
17. O'Donohue, *To Bless the Space*, 192.

We've been using the word transition throughout the book, but O'Donohue contends that a stronger word is needed for such occasions than the word "transition," which to him seems pale, functional, and inadequate.[18] What you are facing with your graduation from seminary is more than a transition. For you, this is a threshold. More than simply an accidental line that separates one place or time from another, a threshold is "an intense frontier that divides a world of feeling from another, a dividing line between the past and the future."[19]

May you cross this threshold worthily. Take a moment to allow that blessing to rest upon you as you cross the threshold from seminary to the rest of your ministry. You are moving from one calling to another. It has been your vocation for the past few years to engage in rigorous, life-giving preparation. Earning a degree is significant, but you have done more than that. While in seminary, you have given yourself over to the inspiration of worship, the support of community, an understanding of the riches and depth of the Christian story, and ongoing introspection and discernment about how you can best respond to God's claim on your life.

To attend seminary is a calling itself. It's related, of course, to your call to ministry, but it's worth lingering on this side of the threshold long enough to recognize the gifts, challenges, and privileges of this time in your life. Whatever excitement you have about finishing your studies and whatever anxiety you have about what comes next for you, pause now for a moment. Offer your gratitude to God and to those with whom you have completed this part of your sacred journey. Bring to your consciousness the best parts of your seminary experience and gather those unto yourself as you prepare for passage.

Your canoe awaits. Ahead for you is a profoundly fulfilling, often joyous, sometimes overwhelming, and occasionally exasperating voyage. You will navigate by nimbleness, practicing curiosity, clarity, agility, proximity, and temerity all along the way.

18. O'Donohue, *To Bless the Space*, 193.

19. O'Donohue, *To Bless the Space*, 192.

Restlessness and resilience are gifts for the journey, never allowing you to become complacent and never leaving you without a way.

May God go with you.

And may you cross this threshold worthily.

Bibliography

Augsburger, David. *Caring Enough to Hear and Be Heard*. Grand Rapids: Baker, 1982.

Bach, Johann Sebastian. "St. John Passion." BWV 245, Aria S.

Baillie, John. *A Diary of Private Prayer*. New York: Scribner, 2014.

Berry, Wendell. *This Day: Collected & New Sabbath Poems*. Berkeley: Counterpoint, 2013.

Biko, Steve. *I Write What I Like: Selected Writings*. Chicago: University of Chicago Press, 1978.

"Billy Collins." https://www.poetryfoundation.org/poets/billy-collins.

Bloom, Matt. "About." http://wellbeing.nd.edu/about/.

———. "Flourishing in Ministry: Emerging Research Insights on the Well-Being of Pastors." https://wellbeing.nd.edu/assets/198819/emerging_insights_2_1_.pdf.

Bono. "Because We Can, We Must." https://almanac.upenn.edu/archive/between/2004/commence-b.html.

Book of Common Prayer. New York: Oxford University, 1990.

Boulton, Matthew Myer. *Life in God: John Calvin, Practical Formation, and the Future of Protestant Theology*. Grand Rapids: Eerdmans, 2011.

Bradbury, Ray. *Zen in the Art of Writing: Releasing the Creative Genius within You*. New York: Bantam, 1990.

Bridges, William. *Transitions: Making Sense of Life's Changes*. Cambridge: Da Capo, 2004.

Brown, Brené. *Daring Greatly: How the Courage to Be Vulnerable Transforms the Way We Live, Love, Parent and Lead*. New York: Avery, 2012.

———. *The Power of Vulnerability: Teachings on Authenticity, Connection and Courage*. Read by the author. Louisville, CO: Sounds True, 2012. Audio book.

Brueggemann, Walter. *Journey to the Common Good*. Louisville, KY: Westminster John Knox, 2010.

Byassee, Jason. *Trinity: The God We Don't Know*. Nasvhille: Abingdon, 2015.

Chalice Hymnal. St. Louis: Chalice, 1995.

Bibliography

Chamorro-Premuzic, Tomas. "Curiosity Is as Important as Intelligence." *Harvard Business Review*, August 27, 2014.

Doctorow, E. L. *Writers at Work: The Paris Review Interviews.* Vol. 8. London: Penguin, 1988.

Galindo, Israel. "Six 'Tells' of A Differentiated Leader." http://www.ctsnet.edu/six-tells-differentiated-leader/.

Gladwell, Malcolm. *Outliers: The Story of Success.* New York: Back Bay, 2011.

Godwin, Gail. *Evensong.* New York: Ballantine, 1999.

Goethe, Johann Wolfgang von. *Maxims and Reflections.* New York: Penguin, 1998.

Heifetz, Ronald, et al. *The Practice of Adaptive Leadership: Tools and Tactics for Changing Your Organization and the World.* Boston: Harvard Business Press, 2009.

Heyward, Carter. *Keep Your Courage: A Radical Christian Feminist Speaks.* New York: Seabury, 2010.

Huber, Jane Parker. *A Singing Faith.* Philadelphia: Westminster, 1987.

Hybels, Bill. *Holy Discontent: Fueling the Fire that Ignites Personal Vision.* Grand Rapids: Zondervan, 2007.

"Jazz Improvisation," https://www.apassion4jazz.net/improvisation.html.

Kincaid, William B. "Mistake: Essays by Readers." *Christian Century*, July 6, 2016.

Koester, James. "Finding God in the Marsh—Br. James Koester." https://www.ssje.org/2010/06/08/finding-god-in-the-marsh-br-james-koester/.

Kumar, Manjit. *Quantum: Einstein, Bohr and the Great Debate about the Nature of Reality.* New York: Norton, 2008.

Leas, Speed. *Discover Your Conflict Management Style.* Rev. ed. Lanham, MD: Rowman and Littlefield, 1998.

"Love Made Me an Inventor." *Faith and Leadership*, September 12, 2011. https://www.faithandleadership.com/love-made-me-inventor.

Manley, James K. "Spirit." *Chalice Hymnal.* St. Louis: Chalice, 1995.

Martin, Mary, vocalist. "The Sound of Music." Composed by Richard Rodgers and Oscar Hammerstein II. 1959.

Milne, A. A. *Winnie-the-Pooh.* New York: Dutton, 1926.

Moseley, Dan P., and K. Brynolf Lyon. *How to Lead in Church Conflict: Healing Ungrieved Loss.* Nashville: Abingdon, 2012.

O'Donohue, John. *To Bless the Space Between Us: A Book of Blessings.* New York: Doubleday, 2008.

Peterson, Eugene. *Pastor: A Memoir.* New York: HarperOne, 2011.

Reis, Eric. *The Lean Start-Up: How Today's Entrepreneurs Use Continuous Innovation to Create Radically Successful Businesses.* New York: Crown, 2011.

Robinson, Marilynne. *The Death of Adam: Essays on Modern Thought.* New York: Picador, 2005.

Scharen, Christian A. B., and Eileen R. Campbell-Reed. "Learning Pastoral Imagination: A Five-Year Report on How New Ministers Learn in Practice." *Auburn Studies* 21 (Winter 2016) 1–61.

Shirey, David. *The Chimes of Central Christian Church.* August 27, 2014.

Smith, Jonathan Z. "The Bare Facts of Ritual." In *Imagining Religion: From Babylon to Jonestown,* 53–65. Chicago Studies in the History of Judasim. Chicago: University of Chicago Press, 1982.

Stafford, William. "Vocation." In *The Way It Is: New and Selected Poems,* 102. St. Paul, MN: Graywolf, 1977.

Suchocki, Marjorie. *God, Christ, Church: A Practical Guide to Process Theology.* New York: Crossroad, 1982.

Sullivan, Andrew. "I Used to Be A Human Being." *New York Magazine,* September 19, 2016.

Thurman, Howard. *The Growing Edge.* Richmond, IN: Friends United, 1956.

Tutu, Desmond. *God Has A Dream: A Vision of Hope for Our Time.* New York: Doubleday, 2004.

Williamson, Marianne. *A Return to Love: Reflections on the Principles of A Course in Miracles.* New York: HarperCollins, 1992.